LAURIE LEE

Village Christmas

And Other Notes on the English Year

PENGUIN BOOKS

PENGUIN CLASSICS

UK | USA | Canada | Ireland | Australia
India | New Zealand | South Africa

Penguin Books is part of the Penguin Random House group of companies
whose addresses can be found at global.penguinrandomhouse.com.

First published in Penguin Classics 2015
006

This collection copyright © The Trustees of the Literary Estate of Laurie Lee, 2015
'My Day' copyright Laurie Lee/*Vogue* © The Condé Nast Publications Ltd

Set in 10.5/13 pt Dante MT Std
Typeset by Jouve (UK), Milton Keynes
Printed in Great Britain by Clays Ltd, St Ives plc

A CIP catalogue record for this book is available from the British Library

ISBN: 978–0–241–24365–7

Contents

Contents

Notes on England

To most of us, England is a green sweep of heraldic history marked here and there by the black thumb of coal. The bit I know best is local and enduring, has little history and almost no official heroes.

I was born in a corner of the Cotswolds – an odd lozenge of land centred round the small town of Stroud, cluttered, iridescent but unchangingly beautiful, comprising a bit of swampy plain, fine secretive valleys and a brooding ridge of bare hills stretching away to Wales and to the blue Wenlock Edge.

I was nineteen years old when I first left my home ground, where all of us at that time, family and neighbours alike, had seemed happily and tightly wedged. 'Ah, the Cotswolds,' people said, when I got to London. 'Stow-on-the-Wold, Bourton-on-the-Water, Burford, eh?' I didn't know any of them. They might as well have been in Lapland. People in our valleys seldom budged very far.

Stroud, Slad, Sheepscombe, Painswick, Bisley, Miserden, The Camp – these were the Cotswolds we knew, the limit of our contentments.

What I loved, and still love, about that small pocket of England was that it was odd, radiant and unlike anywhere else. So static, indeed, and immovable, that our staying put within its boundaries seemed to magnify the qualities of where we were, so that it seemed natural to know every blade of grass, each stone and roof tile.

Our bit of country, because of its extremes – its slopes, shadows, oblique angles of light, deep woods and high open fields – seemed also to separate and dramatically magnify the seasons, the winter landscape locked up with a giant key, great snowdrifts arriving like the tents of Attila; spring too pretty by half with sudden shining streams and beech leaves like fresh-washed salads; summer, a brown exhaustion of baking wheat with cows lying in brown mud round the edges of ponds; and autumn, a fermentation of all that had gone before.

Were these seasons remarkable or did they happen elsewhere? To me they happened only at home. And happening in that place, at that time, have become a reference for all seasons, everywhere, whenever I pause to think of them.

As do those sudden outbursts of oceanic storms, western gales blowing in from the Atlantic, with sheep huddling in bunches, bushes bent to the ground and chimneys toppling, and birds flying backwards; so perpetual were those winds funnelling up my valley that I'd swear, at times, I could smell New York three days old and the overnight street of Cork.

This bit of England was also a country of seepages, shaped and populated by them; seepages from the melting glaciers, the rivers and estuaries, up which my neighbours had arrived in their canoes and coracles, settling, raising cattle, building walls, digging holes, becoming miners, shepherds, weavers. 'Hogg', 'Webb', 'Wynn', 'Jones'; you scarcely needed to open your mouth to speak such names, and with jobs like theirs you didn't move about much. A damp green place this, small and domestic in scale. But the citizens know its measure.

The expansive oddity of this district is that it breaks into three – the high, flat sheep-hills, the valleys dropping to the plain, then across the Severn westward to the black-eyed tribesmen in their forest, each with a private coal mine at the bottom of his garden.

On my side of the river, in spite of the rapid spread of houses and factories muzzling up the valley slopes, you will still see wild animals, in sudden flashes of light, the bright stoat, stumbling badger, the diamond eyes of pheasant and fox; and occasionally, rarely, a red deer fleeing like a curate's daughter.

But overall, it is the scale and timelessness I love – the unblown mystery of this part of England. Trunk roads, TV masts, Berkeley

Nuclear Power Station, yes; but behind us, where the escarpment runs like a long cliff above the plain, up there, outside the villages and above the towns, the little tumps and hillocks still stand in the grass. For three thousand years, the axe, the spade and the plough have carefully circled them and left them untouched.

And beneath the turf they still lie, and we know who they are – grandfathers of our grandfathers whose hazed existence has been carried forward on the living breath of mother to child – the local bronze-age chiefs, squint eyed and laconic, who you still see throwing darts in the pub.

Winter

Village Christmas

Christmas today often falls far ahead of its time, with signs in the shops appearing soon after the summer holidays. But in my childhood, Christmas began at the proper season, only just before the Feast itself.

For us boys in our village in the Cotswolds, it always started on a star-bright night, never prearranged but intuitively recognized. A few of us would wrap ourselves in scarves and mufflers, fix lighted candles in jam jars and go through the streets calling out the rest of the gang. 'Comin' carol-barking, then?' It was a declaration, not a question. One by one they appeared, flapping their arms and stamping their feet.

We were a ragged lot but we had official status, for we were the boys of the village choir, and as a reward for a year of dutiful churchgoing, we'd earned the right to sing carols at all the big houses in the valley, and collect our tribute.

Now our band of musical footpads set off merrily through the crunching snow, swinging out lanterns on loops of string. We began with the Squire, while still in good voice – advancing in awe down his well-swept drive to the great house. The old man, wrapped in a rug, stood at the door and listened, weeping softly, as our Christmas trebles reminded him once more of the passing of time.

After that regal visit, we hurried onward up the valley, calling at the houses of lesser gentry. Beneath frosted windows, in echoing stable yards, under great Gothic porches and in tapestried hallways we sang, eight voices, clear and sweet, ringing out through the winter's night.

'Hark, the herald angels sing!' Once again we were the bearers of the miraculous tidings to house and farm, to the folk by the fire, the stamping beasts in their stalls. And at each house, when we'd finished, we were rewarded with handfuls of coppers, hot mince pies, tangerines – gifts as precious as gold or myrrh.

Next day was Christmas Eve, with preparations at a climax. The kitchen walls shone with reflected snow. Icicles curtained the steaming windows. As soon as we'd finished breakfast the table was cleared for the ceremonial mixing of the pudding – a formal ritual only, for Mother had thoroughly mixed it already, but now each of us had to stir it for luck.

It stood rich and raw in its china basin, packed with currants, raisins, nutmeg, ginger and other musky indefinable spices. We each gave the mixture a solemn stir, made a secret wish, then took a long hard lick at the spoon. I remember well that voluptuous taste of suet and oriental bazaars, together with a faint flavour of pudding cloth.

Christmas in the country meant feasts and fires, a few brief days of excess, when even the poorest among us would confront the stern gods of winter with the bravest possible show of good living. Everybody was busy this morning, chopping wood, carrying in logs or sitting on the doorstep plucking ducks or geese. Now the time had come for us to go up to the woods and collect leaves for decorating the house. Among the black and bare trees we shook the snow from the undergrowth with frost-reddened fingers, seeking the sharp-spiked holly, bunches of laurel and ivy, cold clusters of moon-pale mistletoe. With these, our sisters transformed the familiar kitchen into a grotto of shining leaves, an enchanted bower woven from twigs and branches sprinkled with scarlet berries.

After tea, as darkness fell, we put on our coasts and scarves, and trouped off with Mother to the town several miles down the wind-whipped valley. We always left the buying of our presents to this eleventh hour as part of the season's dramatic crescendo, joining the rest of our neighbours who were all now heading from the shops to catch the last glitter of Christmas Eve. The tiny gaslit stores were gold caverns in the dusk, bursting with festive gods.

We children gazed awhile at the grander toyshops, those with stuffed tigers and life-sized dolls, but ended up as always at Piper's Bazaar, the most magical place in town. In this glittering emporium were presents for all the family: rings, necklaces and brooches for 1d each, tiny tea-sets and dollhouse furniture, tin soldiers, cannons, paints and puzzles, Chinese lanterns and devil masks. For my mother I bought the best in the shop – a brass-framed photograph of Lillie Langtry for 6d. Home again, with the oil lamps and candles lit, we stowed our presents away in the backs of cupboards or behind loose boards in the washhouse.

Later that night, a cousin, who worked in the woods, would leave a splendid Christmas tree at our door. We would haul it inside, plant it in a bucket, and smother it with Chinese lanterns. Mysterious and sparkling, still dripping with melted snow, its feathery branches filling half the kitchen, the tree was our Christmas crown.

Everything was now ready for tomorrow. There was nothing to do except go to bed, curl up in our blankets and wait, each with his long stocking hanging on the bedpost, empty. Would there be a flash of red in the window, a snow-glint of beard and ermine, a whisper of sleigh bells on our rooftops as Father Christmas made his benevolent entrance? We suspended judgment and kept an open mind.

And when it happened, it was like the opening of a flower in the dark, the sudden ripening of fruit on the bough. A minute ago there was just the limp dead stocking. Now it hung heavy, bulging with gifts. Of all moments in childhood this must remain the most haunting, most unforgettable: the drowsy hand in the cold of the winter's dawn reaching out as a test of hope, then suddenly finding itself filled with this weight of love, bestowed silently while it slept.

No matter how early it was, we sat up in our nightshirts, lit our candles, and began our day. Slowly we scattered our treasures across the bedclothes. The biggest toys came first, filling the mouth of the stocking – a clockwork fire-engine whirling with sawtooth cogwheels, followed by a boat, some spotted dominoes and a bright painted humming-top. Here and there among this procession of simple joys we'd find a wrapped bull's-eye, a brazil nut, a russet apple, a couple of figs or a tangerine.

Eager, impatient, yet longing to spin out the moment, we tried not to empty our stockings too quickly. We plunged our hands deeper, searching for the next surprise, trying to guess what it was by touch – hard or soft, sticky, smooth, oblong, round or square. What ecstasies of speculation those fumblings were till one drew forth the object into the light. Then at last one was down to the toe. It was over, that session of unalloyed bliss, like nothing else in life: the slow unwrapping of Christmas in the winter's dawn.

Christmas dressing was formal – for the boys, velvet suits, starched collar, and hair shining with Vaseline; for the girls, best dresses and new pinafores. We tumbled downstairs, three steps at a time, into the kitchen's glow. The fire was ablaze, and Mother had already started the breakfast, frying great pans of eggs and bacon. We sat down to the finest breakfast of the year, which included real cream and porridge.

'Hark, children!' cried Mother, suddenly cocking her head, 'Isn't that pretty? Now fancy that.' With our mouths full of bacon we ran out into the yard and stood listening in the snow. Then we heard it, the pealing of Painswick bells, the traditional and joyous sound, coming faint but clear over the distant hill like icicles stirred by the wind, ringing Christmas in the valley. Our own village bell started up soon after, cool as a snowdrop, calling us all to church. There were no dissenters this morning. Everyone turned out – from the gentry in their carriages to the farmers and their bonneted wives in carts.

For us choirboys there were new robes, cold as sheets of tin, which we donned hurriedly in the shivering vestry. Then with pink cheeks glowing, faces modestly composed, sweets hidden beneath our tongues, we followed the snow-haired vicar to our place in the stalls to a resounding peal on the organ.

'Unto us a Child is born! Unto us a Prince is given!' We sang it full-throated, knowing it to be true.

After a brief sermon, the vicar released us with his blessing and the rest of the day was ours. Back home, we found that Grandpa had come, and a couple of whiskered uncles, all wearing brown polished gaiters.

Eddies of tempting smells filled the crowded kitchen – mince pies, hot pastry, the tang of fresh-chopped parsley, the tingling aroma of the goose, which was too big for the oven and hung turning on a spit before the roaring fire, its fat dripping into a small brass dish. Nothing could be hurried; Christmas dinner was sacred and the waiting was part of its price.

When all was ready at last, the table had never looked more beautiful: the decorated plates, the paper napkins which appeared only once a year, the dishes steaming with vegetables and the little willow-pattern saucers full of dates and nuts and figs. We sat in our places, confidently clutching our knives and forks, knowing that this was one occasion when we could eat our fill, and when there would even be second helpings.

Plates clattered up and down the table, returning laden with helpings of crackling goose. All over the village it would be like this, families gathered for their Feast of the years; proud and flustered mothers giving their star performances, the old and toothless blissfully chewing, the young gorging themselves, grinning fatly at each other, babies in high-chairs sucking marrowbones.

Finally came the climax of the meal – the Pudding – steaming royally on its china dish, a great ball of glory, as black as night, with a bunch of holly twinkling on top. Grandpa fished from his pocket a tiny medicine bottle of brandy, poured it over the pudding and set it alight. Whiskers of pale flame began to purr and flicker around it, dancing over the surface like tremors of lightning.

We all cheered; Mother blushed. 'I hope it boiled long enough,' she murmured. Then she ladled it out with a fiery spoon, a great dollop for every plate. It was the last of the orgy, a surfeit of richness. We searched each morsel for the lucky sixpence, and each child found one, to our astonished delight – the uncles had seen to that.

Christmas dinner over, the elders slumped in their chairs, sipping ginger wine, their voices furry and sentimental. So we left them to doze among the orange-peel and walnuts while we ran out into the snow-filled lanes.

At this hour in the village, mid-afternoon Christmas, only the children seemed to be left alive; the boys trying out their popguns, pelting each other with snowballs, or whizzing up and down on the frozen pond; the girls, more sedate, showing off their bright new ribbons, lace-up boots and rabbit-fur muffs.

Night came early, with the valley and its woods closing in darkly around the house. Now was the time to light the tree, its branches loaded with tinsel, with silver cut-out moons and stars, and with the clip-on candles, each a living tongue of flame, building up a pyramid of dancing light. Mother put out the oil lamps one by one, and we stood hushed and entranced together, adoring the tree and its chaste white glare coated all over in frosty fire.

The precious day was dying. We boys struggled to keep awake, our eyes shadowed like burnt-out candles. How could we leave the beautiful tree? We piled our toys at the foot of our beds and Mother tucked us up, her shadow large on the ceiling, thrown by the beams of a single candle. A long as she was there it was still Christmas, as long as she held the light in our room, the day somehow could not end. We clung desperately to this last moment.

Then Mother left us, and the angle of the candlelight grew narrower on the wall, and finally went out, closing that day forever.

A Cold Christmas Walk in the Country

The women in the kitchen are wrapped in their ritual vapours, having swapped dreamy beds for the clanging hellfires of ovens, spitting bird-roasts, bastings, boiling suds of greens, baked pie-crusts and mysterious stuffings. Distracted but agile they shove me against the wall as I grope to look for my boots. Women preparing a meal, like women at their make-up, inhabit a similar chaos that is not to be tampered with.

'Think I'll take a small walk. Up the road,' I say. 'Past the wood. Down the Pond. I think.'

Spoons flashing in bowls, they raise their heads vaguely as though they'd heard an odd sound in the plumbing. Their eyes look through me but do not see me. I belong to an army of men-in-the-way. I get some raw mince on my fingers, lick it off, wish I hadn't, muffle myself up, and go . . .

Outside there is no surprise in the coldness of the morning. It lies on the valley like a frozen goose. The world is white and keen as a map of the Poles and as still as the paper it's printed on. Icicles hang from the gutters like glass silk stockings and drip hot drops in my hand as I breathe on them.

Taking the air in my teeth I feel the old excitement, the raw echoes of an ancestral world, crammed with bull-headed mammoths and tusk-toothed tigers, of flint spears and boasting in caves. Today is the winter as it always was, and when it wasn't it was not remembered. Forgotten, now, are the small freaks of weather, the offbeat heatwaves and wet-warm Decembers that have cropped up now and then in the past. Winter was always like this since the beginning of winters, since the first man learned to sneeze.

Pushing the cold before me like a sheet of tin, I set off up the Christmas road. I have a new thorn stick with a silver band round it and new gloves with an itchy price tag. Before the New Year I shall no doubt lose the lot. But it doesn't matter, they were made for this day.

It is a morning for heroes and exhilarating exile, a time to shock the blood back to life, while I go stamping frost-footed along pathways of iron, over grass that is sharp as wire, past cottages hollowed out like Hallowe'en turnips all seething with lights and steam.

'Same to you, Miss Kirk!' An old lady totters by, bent double like a tyre round a dartboard. Ancient spirit of the season, she is distributing tea to the peasants, which she has done for the last fifty years. She doesn't have to worry where all the peasants have got to; we all admit to being her peasants today.

I climb up the valley, breathing hard the sharp air which prickles the nostrils and turns to vapour. To be walking today is to be followed everywhere by private auras of pearly cloud. The wandering cows are exhaling too – pale balloons of unheard conversation. The ploughed fields below me have crusts like bread pudding, delicately sugared with twinkling frost. The distant pastures are slivered, crumpled and bare. Even the light they reflect seems frozen.

Where was this valley last summer? It was not here then. Winter and summer are different places. This beech wood, for instance, so empty now, no more than a fissure of cracks in the sky – where is the huge lazy heaving of those June-thick leaves, reeking of sap and the damp roots of orchids, rustling with foxes and screaming with jays and crammed to the clouds with pigeons? The wood, for the moment, is but the scaffold of summer. It stands stripped to the bruising cold. A dark bird or two sit along the bare branches. None of them move. They might be caged.

Approaching the pond at last I notice a sweet smell of ice – or perhaps it is the only memory of it. We could certainly smell ice when we were boys; even in bed, before getting up. One sniff of the air at the moment of waking and one knew whether the pond was frozen, knew the quality of the ice, whether it was rough or smooth, and even (I swear) its thickness.

This morning it is a plate of dark-green glass, wind-polished and engraved with reeds. An astonished swan walks slowly around it, testing the ice for a hole to sit in, then unable to find one it rises up on its webs and flogs the air with its puzzled wings.

Like the wood, the pond is under a spell, silent as a loaded gun, its explosions of moorhens, coots and lilies held in check for a suspended moment. I look through the ice and see tiny bubbles of air bright as lights in a Christmas tree. I see lily leaves, too, frozen solid in bunches. I wonder what the fish are doing . . .

'Come on Eff!' croaks a voice. 'It's froze! Didn't I tell ya?' Two kids have arrived. Tommy Bint and his sister, wrapped in scarves and hot for the ice. They jump up and down and caramels shower from their pockets like nuts from a hazel tree.

'Ain't you goin' on, mister?' Course I'm going on. I test the ice as delicately as the swan. It buckles and groans like an old attic floor but we've soon got a good slide going. All is as it was – the hollow ring of our boots, the panting run and the swooning glide, the brief oiled passage across the face of winter, the magic anarchy of pleasure for nothing.

After an hour we stop, our faces pink as crab apples, a feeling of wings still about our heels. 'Got to get home to dinner. Yummy-yum,' says Tom. 'Baked spuds and a gurt great goose.' 'And fritters,' says his sister. 'And plum puddin' and custard and nobble minces and brizzle nuts and . . . and . . .' 'You'll be sick.' 'I'll be sick.' She goes joyously through the motions. Then they trot off like two rubber balls.

I climb back to the village sliding on frozen puddles. They are like holes of sky in the road. A sudden blackbird alarmed skids out of a bush chipping chains of sharp cries behind him. A true note of winter, like an axe on a tree, a barking dog or a daylight owl – each pure and solitary in the pause of silence from which the past and the future hang.

It has now turned noon and the day slides slowly from the roofs of the sloping village. It freezes harder than ivory; one can almost see it in the air, as though the light was being stretched on nails. A clear cold radiance hangs over the landscape and a crow crosses it on creaking wings. The rich earth, with all its seeds and humming fields and courtships, is now closed and bound in white vellum. Only one colour remains, today's single promise, pricked in red over the ashen world – seen in a flitting robin, some rosehips on a bush, the sun hanging low by the wood, and through the flushed cottage windows the berries of the holly and the russet faces of the feasting children.

It is good to have been walking on such a day, feeling the stove of one's body alive, to be walking in winter on the ground of one's birth, and good to be walking home. The table's laid when I get there. The women are taking off their aprons. It is also good to arrive in time.

My Country Childhood

As Gloucestershire boys, the games and rituals we played seemed to run through the natural order of the seasons. Most games we played for our amusement only; rituals were traditional and sometimes earned us pocket money. At the start of the year we had 'first footing' – crossing a neighbour's threshold early in the morning and wishing them 'Good Luck and Happy New Year!' It was always best if you were the first to call; even better if you had black hair. A 'dark stranger', for some reason, was considered to be symbol of good fortune; those of us with fair hair carried a lump of coal.

With the New Year past came the time of inexhaustible pleasures with the wintry landscapes wrapped up in snow and ice. The generosity of snow always seemed unbounded – you could eat it, drink it, throw it about, make caves or tunnels in it, cut it into slabs, build steps or walls or houses. Country snow always seemed clean and white as paper, so that you could read things in it, track birds, badgers or even foxes, and the big hobnailed boots of your friends. As long as the hard winter lasted, our games were many – playing the xylophone on icicles hanging from the roofs, or licking the same like lollipops; and best of all, if the ice was strong enough, working up a slide across the village pond which, when perfectly polished, was a magic carpet that bore us in an effortless dream through the landscape.

Next, while the frosts still held and the roads were not yet turned to mud, came the time for whipping tops up and down the village – wooden rainbow tops, painted in bright reds and greens. The whips were simple lengths of string or long strips of leather stolen from our sisters' tall lace-up boots. The top was set in the dust, its point screwed in the ground, then whipped sharply so that it flew high through the air. If whipped properly it would settle and spin like a hummingbird, rocking and quivering gently. To keep it alive you ran and whipped it again, and then it would rise singing, and spin even faster, and might strike sparks from the stony road when it landed. On the other hand, it could also sky through a window, or get caught in the whiplash and snap back and give you a bonk on the head.

Later, before the general thaw began, came the time for the bowling of hoops; and these made sparks too when driven along the road, because our hoops were made of iron. I am talking of the days when our roads weren't tarred but were surfaced with little stones and flints. Our iron hoops could strike up brilliant streams of sparks if sent at the proper angles across the stones. They could also be instruments of danger if they got out of control, and could cut open the knee to the bone. But we boys thought no less of them for that and were proud of them for their speed and power. The girls, on the other hand, were only allowed light hoops of cane, which we boys, of course, thought silly.

Many of our games were played in the middle of the roads, which, since there was no traffic in those days – except for an occasional horse and cart, or an old man with a wheelbarrow, were considered a perfectly safe place to be. Here, squatting on our knees in a circle, we played 'knucklebones' or 'five-stones', a game older than Shakespeare, a game of manual dexterity, almost a feat of juggling, fiercely competitive and with many extended variations.

Traditional 'knucklebones' was played with the knuckles of pigs' feet, but as we, for the most part, were too poor to eat meat, we played with little stones instead. The game consisted of tossing the stones in the air, catching them on the back of the hand, manipulating some on the ground while still keeping at least one in the air, grabbing, scrapping and catching until the game was over. The mysteries of 'knucklebones' are too complex to explain fully, unless you happened to be born into them. They require a nimbleness, a sleight-of-hand sufficient to dazzle the eye; and the girls – it must be admitted – were better at it than we were. (But so they were at hopscotch – a game older than the Pyramids).

Summer games were slower but no less carious than others – snail-racing, an indolent pastime; 'French cricket', played along pathways using legs as stumps; warfare with grass-seeds catapulted from the bent looped stem; fishing for tiddlers; and 'fox-and-hounds' in the moonlight.

Then with each autumn came 'conkers' – a classic battle of determination and nerve – with the shiny brown chestnuts hanging on strings and then brutally bashed against each other in turn. Four things could happen in this encounter. Either the striker missed his opponent altogether, or the strings got entangled and caused an awkward pause, or both conkers colliding smashed each other to pieces, or one or other of them emerged victorious. The veteran survivor of many battles took on the value of the conkers he'd vanquished, so that you'd get a 'two-er', a 'twelve-er', even a 'forty-er', according to your various successes. I saw a 'fifty-er' once, a sharp-edged little nut looking grey and hard as a stone. I thought it to be deathless or an invincible destroyer – but some said it had been baked in an oven.

In autumn, too, was the time that we made bows and arrows – perhaps a tribute to the hunting season. Our bows were made of light springy willow, and our arrows cut from a hazel bush, straight peeled and sharpened at the end. If properly strung and used with average skill it was astonishing how powerful these bows and arrows could be, light and far-ranging as those of Persian cavalry or the mounted warriors of the Tartars. At the day's end, I remember, we'd often stand in the blue gloom of the valley and shoot an arrow vertically into the sky, and watch it climb, climb, till it caught the light of the setting sun, and hang there for a moment, gold and illuminated, before turning to plunge back into the evening's shadow. I always think that slender arrow, hanging in the sun's last glow, was the magic symbol of the Fall of the year. Then winter and Christmas would be on us once more, with snowballing and carol-singing, skating and wassailing, and the returning cycle of the seasons, with its ritual games, would begin all over again.

The Lying in State

A cold east wind blows over the roofs of Westminster. The sky is raw and blind. Every flag points westward, a single leaf on a stalk, as if frozen, ready to fall.

Through the comfortless morning treads a mile-long queue, shuffling forward on icy feet, old men and children dressed for naked weather as though approaching some ancient megalith.

Every resounding event seems to be followed by silence, as history catches its breath. So it is this morning in this great bare hall – a silence like a fall of snow, holding the city and the world in a moment of profound reflection, reducing all men to a levelled pause.

The thunder of oratory, the clash of deeds, the head-on collisions of nations, the many thousands of words already spoken about this man, are now halted inside this chamber.

It is a vaulted barn, roofed by Sussex timber, amber-shadowed by its few dim lamps. The harvest is done and the barn seems empty, save for the husk of this mighty seed.

And this, for the moment, is the centre of the world, which no dictator or king could command, a core of sombre radiation and reverberating silence expanding in waves to engage the thoughts of millions.

Those who have waited so long stumble in from the streets, blinking the cold from their snow-flecked eyes. The confrontation is sudden, almost unprepared; the legend too near to be properly focused. Strangely hurried, heads straight, each one files past the coffin in a gentle fluster of emotion. But the scene is lit up as by a flash of dark lightning, instantaneous, never to be forgotten.

He lies on his catafalque, lifted on steps of purple, in a hall built by kings for kings, his coffin wrapped in a flag like a wave of water as if already seaborne for some distant haven.

In this brief and majestic flash of recognition, all men see what their hearts bring with them, just as in life they saw in this kaleidoscope of a man something all of them knew they could be.

For on that shadowed catafalque rests the print of a spirit who when alive seemed to be all things living – who was lover, soldier, artist, wit, master of language and prince of the will, who took fate by the heels and the scruff of the neck and shook it roughly into shape and order, defying its betrayals, indifference and threats, commanding its obedience by obstinacy and bluff, outstaring its mask of disaster till it yielded to victory and danced to the tune he wanted.

This was a man who knew what was possible in men, could touch their nerves with fingers of sulphur, stinging them briefly alive into postures of glory, of sacrifice, suffering and triumph.

It is not sorrow to leave him. For nothing has been lost. This is the shut book of a life completed. A legend to be laid away among those ancestral ghosts who stand guard over a perplexing future.

The winter day darkens. The thousands still come, snow-footed down carpets of silence. The streams divide softly, passing on each side of the bier like water flowing around a rock. Each stream for a moment thins to a single person, alone in his private homage. It seems sufficient to have been here; few glance at the coffin, but gaze ahead as they walk to the exit. Only at the great west door do they pause to look back, their damp eyes sparked by candles – a gesture of almost desperate farewell snatched from the pressure of time, of history, and the crowds behind them. Outside in the winds the other thousands are waiting, their faces pinched and patient. Each one in his turn comes like another candle to the hall. Not since the war has there been such a shared emotion.

Born Survivor

I love the world and all its trivialities, the little domestic details, the post box on the corner, the wet gutters, the leaves, the buses, the sunset.

Sometimes youngsters say: 'I didn't ask to be born.' I didn't ask to be born either. But I'm glad I was.

Because I wrote a book which is often down for GCE in schools, children think I'm dead. Not long ago a girl came up to me when I was sitting outside the village pub and said: 'Excuse me, sir, can you tell me where Laurie Lee is buried?'

When the time comes I shall be buried in the village churchyard. That's where my mother is buried. I share my mother's passionate attachment to this world and all its imperfections.

Knowing that an unbaptized child would be buried in unhallowed ground among the old jam jars, my mother sent for the vicar the day I was born and he christened me that afternoon from a teacup. It was several years before I was officially christened in the church. I could walk by then, made free with the holy water and cheeked the vicar.

Some ancestral toughness, I believe, saw me through that first day. I remained seriously ill for months, never moved, nor cried, just lay where my mother put me, staring at the ceiling, scarcely breathing, in a motionless swoon.

For a year I lay there, prone to many invasions, enough to mop up an orphanage. I had diphtheria, whooping cough, pleurisy, pneumonia, congestion of the lungs . . . I collected minor diseases throughout my childhood – chickenpox, mumps, measles, adenoids, ringworm, nosebleeds, nits, earache, stomach ache, the wobbles, the bends, scarlet fever, catarrhal deafness. I had little red eyes I was so poorly and a steady sniff. The village schoolmistress used to say to me: 'Go outside and sit on the wall and give your nose a good blow.'

I used illness as a weapon. I'd wake in the morning and say I couldn't go to school because I'd got the wobbles, couldn't walk – and in the afternoon be as fresh as a daisy. Yet I could be a great walker when I was a boy – three miles to school and three miles back. Sometimes I'd get a stitch. There was one cure for that. You put your foot up on a milestone and kissed your knee. It always worked.

I have never had a chance to talk about my health before. Nobody wants to hear about your illnesses. All they're interested in is your holiday snaps.

When I was young I had an operation for my sinus at St Thomas's Hospital in London. There I was recovering from this rather nasty operation with headache, toothache, earache; I was in agony. Yet when friends rang to inquire how I was they were told I was comfortable. I had never been so uncomfortable in my life. I felt rather like a man who was kicked by a horse whose condition was described as stable.

I went back to St Thomas's Hospital once with a hangover. I was only passing by and wanted a couple of aspirins. But they said I'd have to stay in for observation, wheeled me into a room and said 'I'm terribly sorry but you've got a thrombosis of the leg.' And I had two operations.

I have had a terror of medical authority – doctors, dentists, hospitals, medical opinions – since childhood. I always think: Please don't let me fall into their hands. Let me be born at home, stay at home, die at home.

I don't write like Jeffrey Archer – on a word processor called Priscilla. I love manipulating words. It's very rewarding when you've done it. But it does take so much out of you. I'm prone to scrambling of the brains, can only survive a couple of days a week. Then I have to draw the blinds to regain my strength. You can talk about broken bones and car accidents. But you can't talk about what happens to the brain and nervous system when you're writing at that level.

My theory is that a strong healthy man isn't likely to be creative. It is illness and pain that encourages him to live another life.

I still get this recurrent pneumonia when the lungs are full of pulsating barbed wire and the temperature goes up. When that happens I hide away like an animal in the long grass or bushes. The only cure is to lie still and wait for it to pass. Sometimes it takes a couple of days, sometimes two weeks. But it does make you turn your attention to the reality of having to leave this world one day and if I ask myself if I'm reconciled, the answer is I'm not.

Now I've got a split iris, can't read as easily as I could. But I can still see landscapes and girls' legs.

The Fight to Save Slad

When I gaze across Slad Valley from my cottage window, I can see – despite my fading sight – fields and hedgerows that were planted a thousand years ago. Beyond my garden is a honey-coloured Cotswold-stone farmhouse with the date 1521 carved in the wall in old-fashioned script. To the right is a sixteenth-century house with perfect Elizabethan windows.

There's a field halfway up the slope and when the sun is sinking in autumn it throws a special slant and shadow and reveals the foundations of an ancient manor house and the line of the old vanished road running down to the stream.

There's also Swift's Hill, crouching like an almost pagan presence, protecting the valley. In fact, one of my ancestors was buried there three thousand years ago. At least, when archaeologists dug him up I claimed him as an ancestor because a dentist friend who examined him told me his teeth were just like mine.

I had hoped that this beloved landscape of hollows and silence and bullying autumn winds, the inspiration for my book *Cider with Rosie*, might long outlast me. Yet this week I had to drag myself from my sickbed to add my rather quavery voice to those of my campaigning neighbours. We want to stop a new housing estate being built in our valley.

This irreplaceable patch of English countryside is often referred to as the 'Cider with Rosie Valley' or 'Laurie Lee's Valley' because I had the great good fortune to be born and raised here, and because I 'immortalized' it, as media types say, in my book about Slad life at the start of this century.

But it is not 'my' valley. It belongs to everyone who loves

unspoiled green landscapes and to all those not yet born, and in a way is a symbol of much of what is happening to Britain.

And so I stood up at the meeting of local people, wrapped in a blanket and trying to stifle a hacking cough, and pointed out to the gathered property speculators that Slad Valley is a pure, refreshing artery which pours crystal air and unpolluted nourishment into Stroud, and that if we allow their so-called development to go ahead we shall see our rural landscape scarred forever and will be guilty of a self-inflicted wound that not even time will heal.

Everyone clapped and nodded their heads apart from a youngish Maggie Thatcher lookalike who was surrounded by piles of statistics. She was there representing the developers and, in a musical but threatening voice, she gave us protesters a severe dressing down.

She seemed to be saying, if I interpreted her words correctly, that the proposed development of ninety houses, roads, roundabouts, car parks and so forth had been approved at government level and there was nothing that ordinary people could do about it. My neighbour muttered that there was nothing we could do either when developers closed down our bus station.

On that occasion we'd been suddenly 'privatized' and a comfortable place where people could sit, gossip and buy cups of tea had been demolished. Where we'd once had four buses a day dropping off the old-timers when they tapped the driver on the shoulder, we now have about two buses a week, and people are jostled about in the rain and tumble into the gutter in the stampede to clamber aboard. There are no buses at all to some villages.

I told the chairwoman that the word 'development' is just a euphemism for ravagement and exploitation, and that the so-called developers are not building a housing estate for the fun of it but to screw as much profit out of it as they can. Everyone clapped again and stamped their feet in agreement.

The meeting hall was full, not just with troublesome old narks like me, but with young mothers, teenagers, fathers, lovely old ladies being guided into their seats by the elbow – all of us respectable, decent citizens wishing to preserve our landscape of tangled woods and sprawling fields, of steep, grassy slopes that are a funnel for winter winds and a bird-crammed, insect-hopping suntrap in summer.

When the statistics lady repeated that the Government's decision was final, I called out 'Never trust the Government. Look what they did to the coal mines', and in doing so I no doubt spoiled forever my chances of a knighthood . . . but I am extremely angry.

This valley has remained untouched since Roman times, and a housing estate will mean the end of a pastoral paradise that generations have loved and grown up in. Repeated in other valleys all over the country, it would destroy our landscape.

I must emphasize that I am not against people having the right to a decent home, but I do think estates should fit in with the existing environment. We can't understand why the developers don't move into the centre of Stroud – a town which is very dear to me – much of which has sadly become corroded and empty, with boarded-up shops and smashed windows, and redevelop what is already there.

Further up the valley is Bulls Cross, a saddle of heathland where relics of the old stagecoach roads are still imprinted in the grass, and below that is a dank yellow wood known locally as Deadcombe Bottom.

Here it was, years ago, that my brothers and I discovered a cottage with roof fallen in and garden run wild. We played there often among its rotten rooms and gorged ourselves on the sharp apples which hung round the shattered windows. We could do what we liked there and it was only later that we learned it had been the home of the Bulls Cross hangman and that he had hanged himself there on a hook in the hall which we liked swinging from.

As a child I thought the whole world was like Slad Valley. Until I was eighteen I'd never travelled more than two miles. I thought Tewkesbury was in Poland.

This week the valley I love is loud and alive with spring birdsong, but the moment the bulldozers move in the birds will shut up and the soul will fly out of Slad. Housing development will gradually encroach upon the fields, woods, lanes and quarries which were an open-air playground for me and generations of children, and a setting for unforgettable adventures and encounters with badgers, rabbits, birds' nests, glow-worms.

It was in these meadows where I first breathed the first faint musks of sex and where Rosie Burdock shared her cider with me during haymaking, on a motionless day of summer, hazy and amber-coloured, with the beech trees standing in heavy sunlight as though clogged with wild, wet honey – a day when the hay-wagon under which we lay went floating away like a barge out over the valley.

A new housing estate built here will simply open the floodgates; development will creep up the valley, blotting out fields where youngsters now prowl and run at liberty. Children trapped in new concrete estates will be denied the freedom we knew. They'll become prisoners of television, as most children are today, and as they grow up they'll start hanging about the streets in gangs and stealing cars.

When I left Slad to walk to Spain, and subsequently travelled to forty different countries, I realized that nothing could equal this valley for loveliness. I also knew that I would have to come back.

When I took Cathy, my child bride as I like to call her, to Spain in 1950, I pined for Slad. We were then so poor that we lived on plain spaghetti and chopped up the furniture for firewood.

For twelve years we were disappointed at not having a child. Then, when I made enough money from my first book, *A Rose for Winter*, we returned to Slad. A year later our daughter Jessy was born and I truly believe that we had to come back home in order to get her.

Slad is where I belong. A few years ago, when I was in America for Christmas, a friend gave me a painting he had done of the Slad Valley. My eyes immediately filmed over and I wanted to drop everything and leg it back home.

So what can we ordinary people do to save our countryside for future generations? Well, six years ago, when developers were planning to chop down twelve ancient trees to make way for a new

Tesco supermarket in Stroud, a lot of people protested by climbing up into the trees, and I wrote a little joke verse that went:

'I think that I shall never see
A Tesco lovely as a tree
And if we are forced to cut ours down
'Twill shame the gateway to our town.'

It wasn't one of my best but the trees were saved, and I like to believe that passionate public opinion can influence the most stony-hearted ministers.

Of course, I am now an old man, but this fight to save Slad is a very serious matter. I'd like to know that those who come after me can sit on the hill overlooking the valley and know exactly where the sun and moon will rise, and from behind which tree, while the year goes through its changing phases as it has done down all the centuries.

Spring

The English Spring

Almost every place in the world knows some measure of spring – a moment's thaw, a brief changing of gears, perhaps a pause in the furnace of some desert wind, a burst of rock-flowers, a revving-up of the blood.

But spring comes to England as to no other country, as though this island were its natural home, as though this small green platform on the edge of the Atlantic was the original spawning ground of the season. Indeed you might almost imagine, to judge from much of our folklore and poetry, that Spring and England had invented each other.

For one thing it seems to last longer here, lingering voluptuously over the passive landscape, like the trembling wing of some drowsy bird stretched in a trance and loath to leave it. The Mediterranean spring can be brash and violent, an explosion of growth that withers in a week. But spring in England is like a prolonged adolescence, stumbling, sweet and slow, a thing of infinitesimal shades, false starts, expectations, deferred hopes, and final showers of glory.

The first intimations come as early as January, several months ahead of their time, when a sudden breath of warm air can release a quick prelude of birdsong, valiant but half-deceived – the throbbing cry of a blackbird like a rising arrow, or the low fat call of a dove. Perhaps the sky very briefly turns from grey to rose, clouds break to a southern light, and the soft changes in the air make one pause in the street, unclench one's fists, look up, remember.

But these signs are the outriders, the single spies, scouting ahead of the big battalions. Winter hardens again and settles back on the world. There are dark weeks to be lived through yet. But the promise has been made, and the blackbird repeats it, in brief snatches, in the teeth of the cold.

February is zero, twenty-eight days of waiting, a month of silence and frozen growth, when all the germs of spring stand on the brink of stillness, life loaded but as yet unfired. The tight buds of the trees hang like polished bullets ready-poised for the sun's first spark. Roots are buried fuses, set for the detonations of petals; fields stand stripped for the first green flame. It is a month when all life huddles in a carapace of ice, in a shell of necessary impatience.

Then almost overnight comes gusty March and the first real rousing of spring – a time of blustering alarms and nudging elbows, of frantic and scrambling awakenings. It is a bare world still, but a world of preparation and display against the naked face of the countryside. The cold east wind puts an edge to activity. Hares dance in the shivering grasses. Rooks load their loud nests on the bending treetops and the wild duck mates in the reeds.

There is a fierce drive now in the antics of the earth, a hint of fire in the moving air. Giant combs stir the woods, shaking out catkin and pussy willow – the golden first flowers of the trees – and the birds no longer hop singly about, or brood mutely under the bushes, but suddenly take wing and chase each other, clamouring with new intentions.

March is the time of spring's first hot certainties, melting the winter's sleep around us, when the dawn songs of these birds, robin, blackbird and thrush, are like drops of warm oil in the dark, liquid sounds that pour softly upon our deadened senses, healing us back to life. The early flowers, too, just appearing in the woods, pointed periwinkle, anemone, violet, are sharp tiny stars on the cold black ground, sudden cracks in the earth's big freeze.

The earth tilts, the graph rises, the first profits are gathered, bolder statements are made in the air. There is an extension of light at both ends of the day, more health in the face of the sun. Buds are swelling, cows fattening, farmers ploughing their fields, cottagers turning the clods in their gardens; cocks crow, hens lay, the pond is cloudy with frogspawn – you know at last things are going to be all right.

March is the wild time, the preliminary attack, the great lion that claws at the roots – then shading away into April, all fury spent, its shaggy head laid between its paws.

And April, indeed, is the lamb of spring, the Paschal Lamb of resurrection, which walks through the burgeoning English landscape in the pure coat of its Easter wool. White is the colour now, with honeyed pyramids in the orchards and drifts of thorn-flowers like snow in the hedges, where the first slow bees, still aching with cold, come fumbling to unlock the petals.

T. S. Eliot called April 'the cruellest month', and it is the month of spring's sweetest pain – the pain of awakening and having to live once more after the anaesthetic of winter, the agony of sap returning to the limbs, of numb hands held to the fire. It is also the pain of Lazarus called back from the tomb, the sudden end to sleep and forgetting, the pain of groping shoots and uncurling emotions, of being shaken again with love.

But this is also the splendour of English April, its blinding shock and light, with everything suddenly fresh-peeled and shining with the vaporous brilliance of the newly born. The enlarged blue skies pulse with showers and sunshine, clouds are lively as kicking babes, while the tender new radiance washes down from the heavens purging the world of the wastes of winter.

Between the showers of April even the sunlight is wet, a moist gold like transparent honey, mistily dripping across the hills and valleys and filtering into the damp warm depths of the woods. The fatty gold of this sun seems to cover the ground so that all the flowers become pieces of it, the yellow crocus and celandine, the first marigold in the marsh, the butterpat primrose and daffodil. Later the mysterious bluebells collect in pools, deep and still in the forest shadows, fringed by opening ferns and the bitter ivy, blank as the eyes of witches.

April's resurrection is the holiest of times, the dressing of the goddess of earth, as the sharp new green powders the edge of the woods and the first skylark runs his song up the sky. All the birds are nesting, crouching on jewelled little eggs and packing the bushes with feathers; the swallow returns, swooping from Africa;

the cuckoo gives his first warm shout of the year; windows are thrown open, new hats bloom on housewives, and lovers at last are reacquainted with grass.

English April is also the sign of the first spring festivals, as old as man's life on earth, with the worship of the green, the celebration of birth, of salvation and the open air. Lent was a period of fasting, almost of fear, a placating of the hidden sun; but with the arrival of Easter, man comes out of his shelter, looks about him, and doubts no more.

All the pagan anxieties that still sit in our bones, locked there through the English winter, by shackles of cold and by lack of light, are assuaged on this happy morning. Curious rites and demonstrations, vestigial and confused, filtering down from who knows what distant shores – from Palestine, Rome, Ancient Greece or Egypt – still survive or are remembered here.

The townsman, though shorn from his ancient roots, still feels the thrust of spring through the pavements, grows restless, smartens up, repaints the front of his house, plants some seeds in his window box, or joins his neighbours in the streets for the first ritual washing of cars before the first drive to the crowded sea. In the country, of course, the memory is stronger, with nature a more overwhelming presence, where the spring gods of our forefathers, though now grown dim, still haunt us with primeval dreams.

I was born and brought up in the west country of Gloucestershire, a place of steep hills and secret valleys, and the spring customs I've heard about, or took part in as a child, were once common throughout the whole of England. At Easter, there was the usual giving of eggs, ancient emblems of life and fertility, the customary glut of white weddings, the bleaching of choirboy's robes, the decorating of the church in the first of the green. There are still, even now, the rituals centred on water – the blessing of wells by flower-decked children; and the annual outing to the Severn to see the big spring tide, awesome symbol of regeneration, which coincides with the moon and comes roaring upriver with the mighty thrust of a god.

But I can remember, or have heard the old folk describe, stranger rites that at last are dying, the local acting of myths whose mysterious origins reach back beyond recognition. Each parish, each village, each tribal family seemed to perform some special variation of its own. What they meant, where they came from, no one seemed to know; and in the old days would not have asked.

For instance, there was that curious Easter dance performed at a village a few miles from my home, when the entire population, holding onto each other's coattails, wound like a serpent through the narrow streets. It was called 'Threading the Needle', and was done every year, though nobody could remember why. What was its meaning? The drive of sap through the roots, of living blood through the veins of the village, or some old tribal wandering through the chambers of the underworld before emerging into the light of spring?

The village stands on a hill beside an Iron Age camp built over three thousand years ago. The original settlers, they say, came from the eastern Mediterranean – and clearly their children are still here today. For looking at the old photographs of the dance, showing the various local families dressed in their country suits of holiday – Mrs Gardner and Mrs Cook, in their Victorian poke bonnets, kicking up their heels behind their prancing husbands – I have often wondered at the mystery they were celebrating, whether it might be older than the camp itself, whether perhaps these neighbours of mine were continuing the step of a dance first learned by their ancestors in the labyrinth of the Minotaur.

The Needle dance was peculiar to that village, as though its people were a cut-off tribe. But just across the valley, on the hilltop opposite, they observed a quite different custom. Here, at Easter, they elected a Mock Mayor for themselves, again a strictly local affair, which took place with that mixture of horseplay and pomp which often marks the grave of a once sacred rite. The elected Mayor was usually of humble origins, perhaps a well-muscled carter or blacksmith – a substitute – who knows? – for the mock king of the ancients, the tribal corn god or fertility hero. In the old days, of course, the village would have cut his throat, and scattered his blood to renew the crops. Over the centuries, however, they had grown less rough with their hero, and carried him about in an old chair instead. First, the Mayor was enthroned at the edge of the horsepond and treated with homespun reverence, decorated with flowers and surrounded by psalm-singing villagers, while he splashed their faces with water. Then he was borne through the village to the music of fife and drum playing 'See the Conquering Hero Comes!', ending with a slap-up feast at the local tavern – called significantly The Rising Sun.

This was, after all, in the country at least, the true time of the year's beginning, with the new-sprung green, the return of the sun, the yeast of the Easter rising. Nothing else in the year was so important as this, dramatically balanced between fear and hope, recalling the need in the countryman for a recourse to ancient magic, propitiation, and, at last, rejoicings. Around my Gloucester-shire hills this was the common theme, scattered with variations throughout the villages. Then, with Easter gone, came the First of May, and perhaps the greatest Feast of them all.

The month of May in England, so long awaited, is the flower-studded crown of spring, the final raising of the curtain on all we'd been promised, the shimmering threshold to the mansions of summer. Everything, suddenly, begins to happen at once; the woods are brilliant as new-washed salads, mornings are clear as water, skies soft as wool, and nature gives a loud green shout of abundance.

'Going a-Maying, then?' we used to ask each other. We'd walk through the fields at dawn, taking great gulps of the milky air, and counting the flowers in the grass. It was spring, they said, when a barefooted maid could tread on seven daisies at once. Our sisters soon proved it, ripping off shoes and stockings; then scrubbed their cheeks in the dawn-wet grasses – that cheap and traditional beauti-fier of spring, said to endow one with eternal youth.

May the First was for May-walking, for choosing the May King and Queen, and for the setting up of those ribboned maypoles (con-demned by Cromwell's Puritans as 'those stinking idols, round which they do leap and daunce, like heathens'). It was also the occasion for gathering flowers and branches and for bearing them home in triumph: bluebells, buttercups, buckets of cowslips for wine, wood sorrel, cranesbill, cuckoo-flowers; scented shaves of wild fruit-blossom coated with drunken moths, crab apple, cherry and sloe – anything, that is, except the ashen bloom of the black-thorn, which meant death to the head of the house.

Once upon a time nobody worked on May Day, it was the year's great holiday from labour, when man straightened his back from his crouched servitude to the soil, his wife left her cave-like hovel, and all stepped forth to join with their neighbours as temporary princes of the earth. In fields golden with dandelions and buzzing with larks, this was their one short day without care, dedicated to ceremonies reflecting those pre-Christian rites that came to England with the first handful of seed-corn.

May Day was the time, particularly in my part of the country, when the people went to the hills, to the sheep-bitten ridges of ancient turf among the encampments and tombs of their ancestors. Here almost everyone came early to see the May sun rise, as though to meet it halfway in welcome, and then to spend the free day as their fathers had, in a semi-pagan rough-and-tumble. The hills were their altars, lifted close to the sky, away from the valley's shadows and mud, or were stages raised up to the face of the sun to witness a thousand different kinds of pageantry.

There was the hill, near Gloucester, where the young men of the parish used to fight a battle between winter and summer, ending always in victory for the boys in green, crying: 'We have brought the summer home!' On another hill, nearby, the village turned out in strength to slay a mock dragon – 'the flyin' addard of darkness' – which came out of the river with horrible groans, and was said to be Welsh in origin. Elsewhere there would be cheese-rolling, foot-racing, wrestling, and the lifting of giant stones. The May games on the hilltops were a kind of village Olympics, out of which the year's new heroes were made.

One of the most famous of these was probably the Cooper's Hill Wake, held a few miles from where I was born – a gathering of immense antiquity, combining a radiance of ritual with galumphing country frolics. It began at dawn when the Master of Ceremonies appeared alone on the summit of the hill, a shining figure of light, dressed in a white linen smock and adorned with ribbons of all colours of the rainbow. He must have looked like Lucifer, son of the morning, standing on the hilltop in the early sun, his staff raised high to announce the start of the games, a wreath of flowers about his head.

The games were old and rugged, and so were the prizes; the programme would be nailed to a tree: '2 cheeses to be run for. Some herrings to be dipped for. 1 plain cake to be jumped in a bag for. A belt to be wrestled for. Sets of ribbons to be danced for. A bladder of snuff to be chattered for by old wimmen . . .' After which there'd be dancing to the fiddle of Gypsy Jack and to the tambourine of his black-haired wife, several hours of hard drinking, with men 'grinning through horse-collars', ending with bare-fisted fights down the hillside.

Spring in England, today, may be less robust, with the motor car replacing the maypole. And many of these village ceremonies, unbroken for three thousand years, may at last be fading out. But not all of them, by any means, for some are still kept alive in the games of the country children. Children are the original primitives, the conservative wards of tradition, who act out our racial memories. (It could also be that society, grown doubtful of magic, but unable to ignore it completely, still uses its children as a kind of wry-faced insurance against the possible wrath of the gods.)

In any case, it was the children, when I was a boy, to whom the spring rituals most clearly belonged. It was we who went May-walking, kept the superstitions, turned telephone poles into maypoles, decorated chosen little girls with drooping daisies, and climbed the hilltops to wrestle for prizes. In some of these actions we were encouraged by our elders – those who once would have taken part – the village priest and grown-ups, who stood aside and watched us, like tourists observing the natives.

Just as today, I, too, watch the children of my village intent on their ancient games, and feel the flicker of that original magic, the shafts of light that once raced through my bones, see in the running boys the white harts of the forest, in their combats the defeat of winter, and in some small grubby girl, with her sheaf of limp wild flowers, smiling Flora returned to earth.

For the long English spring, rising to its peak of May, is still a conquering power in our lives. In spite of rubber, concrete and insulations of asphalt, we are not cut off from it yet. Its revolution each year transforms the face of our world, changes the sky, shakes our very roots. Its fragile intensity is one of the miracles of the land, rocking us again with disquiet and rapture, thawing out for a while even the frozen heart, and warming its pulse to the beat of poetry.

A Place on Earth

Most of the gardeners in my village have powerful ankles, even legs of different lengths, for the place lies scattered down the slope of a valley and many of its gardens are steep as roofs. But there are just a few, belonging to the older cottages, that are somewhat more fortunate, having been levelled and terraced in distant days when time and labour were cheap.

My cottage belongs to this luckier group and has one of the flattest gardens in the valley – long, rectangular, almost austerely simple, bounded neatly by limestone walls.

I came to the cottage in early autumn. The previous owner, an indestructible old lady who had been impatiently waiting to die, had grown bored with waiting and suddenly gone off to the seaside leaving all she possessed behind. She sold me everything – the cottage, its furniture, her family photographs, Bibles and texts, cupboards of hand-sewn linen and a shed full of worm-eaten spades.

The cottage itself was still a going concern, still warm as it were from her presence. But not so the garden; this was a ruined blank, a chaos of antique vegetables – huge crumbling cabbages, onions and spinach knotted into a Bolivian hell.

The whole of the garden appeared to have been planted some ten years earlier in a moment of hungry panic, but either the alarm had subsided or the old lady gone off her greens, for the crops had never been gathered. The self-seeded spinach was like elephant grass, the onions tall as street-lamps, and the monstrous cabbage seemed to be shot through with shrapnel, yet immortal, like something from Mars.

It was virgin territory, profuse and disordered, the best foundation for building a garden; no previous design to inhibit one's schemes, no extravaganzas one might feel forced to correct. It could also be said that I was as virgin as the garden, so our potentialities were equal, for though I'd lived in this village for the first twenty years of my life, I'd never gardened before. At our other cottage my mother was the gardener; a dominating impresario, who ordered the earth to bloom with a royal wave of her hand.

Exploiting that early example I now set to work to clear this matted rectangle. I began by burning the arbour and all the vegetables – and the village coughed for days. Then I dug the whole area to a depth undisturbed for perhaps several generations. Bushels of broken clay pipes were turned up by my spade, china dolls' legs, teapots, knucklebones, old coins and cutlery, pots and pans, silver shoe buckles, shattered goblets . . . It was slow, entertaining, head-down sort of work, reaching back to the roots of Genesis, each turn of the spade releasing syllables of the past and the loamy smell of a long-stored fertility.

Finally I was left with a space of lumpy earth, divided down the middle with a box-hedged path – walled, geometrical, and with a gentle, monotonous slope.

After pondering some time what I should do with it I decided to enclose it further, for though walled, it was particularly exposed to the village, which overhung it like a kind of grandstand. All day jolly voices called out from the banks above, confirming one's every action. 'Doing a bit of digging, then?' 'Taking it easy, I see.' 'Tea in the garden? Some folks is lucky.' That bankside wall presented no problem, so I began to raise it up, first with quick-clambering roses, rocketing sunflowers and eight-foot hollyhocks.

Next I planned to relieve the monotony of the ground by breaking and varying its levels: raising the borders near the cottage, laying irregular lawns, and planting trees. The cottage faces the length of the garden and stands low on ancient foundations.

From the ground floor, at first, the view was short and rough: merely a close-up of the dripping vegetables. In their place I raised an extended flower-bed, tilted towards the ground-floor windows, with a path driving through it like a railway cutting along which a more distant prospect was visible.

These borders I terraced with dry-stone walls, using stones from a local quarry. They are the perfect framework for a Cotswold garden, their fossilized surfaces full of warm reflections, on which clinging plants and grasses seem to find a second nourishment and glow even brighter when seen against them.

In laying the croquet lawn I was both Crusoe and Friday, forced to employ my own wits and sinews. The old vegetable patch had to be levelled and rolled, but I possessed neither roller nor wheelbarrow. So I used instead the bottom drawer of a cupboard, with a harness tied to the handles. This could be filled up with earth at the top of the slope and then dragged down and emptied at the bottom, and being heavily loaded, served as both roller and wheelbarrow – a device which might have pleased the Egyptians.

Having next scattered the grass-seed, I watched the birds arrive, which they did in storms of hunger. Freelance bird-scarers, of course, were also short in the district, so the only answer was to build one of my own. I tied some noisy tin plates to a zigzagging clothes-line and led the end through my study window. With the rope tied to my desk I could give it an occasional jerk without interrupting my work – a long-distance tug which rattled the plates in the garden and kept the birds' nerves on edge.

Once the lawn was established I found that it swept the eye to an anticlimax at the end of the garden – the rhubarb patch, the broken wall, and the neighbours' flying washing. I screened this by planting some Michaelmas daisies, another clump of eight-foot sunflowers, a trellis of Sander's White roses, and a *Clematis montana* trained up a strategic clothes-post. To these I added an old stone urn (a relic of a local manor) designed to stand like a bowl of perpetual fire, full of geraniums, against the tropical rhubarb.

The next stage in the break-up of the comparative severity of the garden was to scatter small trees around, so I began with a trailing willow, a white lilac and a cherry, and a peach set against a wall. The planting was a ritual, accompanied by stomping feet and the pouring of wine on the roots. (I had no wine for the willow, so used salad oil instead, from which the tree has only just recovered.)

Having set the garden in motion, started the roses to ramble, and given the borders their first year's bulbs, I then tackled the front of the cottage – a square of old limestone fretted with four small mullioned windows. At first it was bare, save for an ancient climber that had withered to a cat-like claw. This I nervously pruned, then added an Albertine by the porch, a white clematis on the other side, stuck in a shoot of wild honeysuckle under one of the windows and put a wisteria by the southern corner.

This done, I sat back to watch the slow green fire lick its way up the side of the house, to smother the porch and blot out the windows as traditionally it was supposed to do.

That was three years ago; but even a cottage garden they say needs seven before its roots are happy. Even so, I feel mine to be settled, having already taken its future shape. The face of the cottage is already half-embowered, a shaggy banner of tangled creepers. This is the high green altar, while the rest of the auditorium is walled by pink and white roses, climbing up pillars or spread on trelliswork, and over-topped, here and there, by the sunflowers.

These walls, with the cottage, form the four enclosures, between which the garden gently riots. There are now two lawns, at slightly different levels, patches of calm among the flowers.

These are chosen from memories of other cottage gardens, before the seed catalogue introduced its other excesses – the hybrid freaks and other Latinized fancies, neon-hued or mottled like ulcers. Early snowdrops, violets, crocuses and tulips are followed by equally simple though rampant colonies – pansies, snapdragons, sweet williams and petunias.

Later still, at the very height of summer, the creeping ground-fire of the nasturtium takes over, pouring its molten tendrils into every crack and crevice, licking up drainpipes, posts and walls, even climbing the stems of the standing roses and lying hotly among their blooms.

I prefer this vigorous and native anarchy to a more careful

regimentation, that which sets things in rows, at graduated heights, like bored children at a school inspection. I wish for no hothouse exotics, no brisk changes of display brought from the nursery every second week. The pansies, snapdragons, petunias and nasturtiums continue to flower from May till October, are a constant presence, a slow-mounting tide, an impression of eternal summer.

Apart from these and the roses, I have taken up some of the space on the grass by setting flower-tubs around on benches, which stand high and can be moved about at will, altering vistas or masking blank corners. A lofty tub of geraniums, in the right position, can be a Lucifer of morning, catching the early sun above the long low shadows and lighting the day's first fires.

I must think of my garden without delusion; there really is not very much to it. Confined, it cannot hope to be a landscape but at best a pillared and roofless temple. It is new and small, but its face is formed and begins to look beautiful to me; a kind of beauty that is sometimes difficult to share – like showing the neighbours one's holiday snaps. Yet that homegrown rose, though only a rose to others, remains for oneself a miracle of personal godhead.

And there are the other private and indestructible pleasures which one can only know alone the continuous mornings, going out before breakfast to examine each plant for minute advances; the flattery of the bees visiting one's own sown flower; the bird resting in one's planted tree; and the hours bent down, working over the garden's face, close-up, at child-level once again.

Such a simple obsession may be the refuge of one's years, the desire to keep a finger in time, a brief hand in creation, to play a minor god, or even to come to terms with death. I only know that small as my garden is I again have a living root, that even for me something can come to perfection; that I still have a place on earth.

Spring Comes to Slagtown

Forswearing, for once, the usual fragrant haunts of the season – the primrose banks of Sussex, or the daffodil fields of Newent and Grasmere – I went to meet Spring in a most unlikely region; the soot-choked valleys of Slagtown, in the north country.

I found it, of course; but cloaked in the most curious disguises, both fascinating and forbidding. It was as though someone had smothered Sandro's *Primavera* in a suit of coal-tarred overalls – yet left the blue eyes clear.

I went up from London in a train the colour of an ash-cart, riding a dingy wagon whose condition was my first intimation of the land to which I was heading. The southern morning was bright and lively, suburban gardens jingled with flowers and washing, the home-county fields were sharp with growing wheat, woods and copses hung tassels of golden palm, were white with blackthorn, and brilliant with breaking buds. And the sun lay smooth and gentle over all.

Lulled by the warmth of train and landscape, somewhere – not far from Rugby – I fell asleep. I slept long and dreamed deeply of parrots and tropic jungles. Then suddenly I awoke to find I was chill and stiff, and that my parrots were lodged in the throat of an old man sitting beside me, a man who, wracked with coughing, squealed and squeaked like a birdhouse. I wiped the steam from the carriage windows and peered forth. I saw that we were no longer among the gentle fields of the south. We had arrived in Slagtown – and a nether world.

When I left the station – a building squat and black as a fireless grate – it took me some time to get my bearings. Where was the sun? and where the spring? I set off and wandered through the outskirts of the town and at first saw nothing but the chaos, rubbish and sediment of centuries of industrial processes, which had turned these Lancashire valleys inside out. The land was flayed, pocked and pitted; it smoked with the dull residue of a thousand drawn furnaces, it stank with the acid wastes of gigantic chemical actions. Every blade of grass and every possible green thing seemed as impregnated with soot as a flue-brush. What chance had spring here? Surely this was underground, the land of Pluto, with Persephone ever chained beside him?

Yet, no, the sap was rising – though at first I didn't know where to look for signs of it. The sap was rising, not through the boles of willows or flowering chestnuts, but through eyes and talk, gestures, and the games of boys.

But first, before I could see this, I had to work through the outward crust and digest the metallic exterior of this inky world. It was all new to me. Wherever I looked was corruption and smouldering saturnine eruptions. Mountains of slag and slate, like pagan pyramids, shuttered the sky and buried within their heaps a hundred years of light and labour. A derelict bridge of purple brick stepped from one hill to another, the archaeological ghost of some bankrupt highway, its visage bearded with weed and grime. On every hand, raggedly welded together, stood grey-walled factories, with fierce black chimneys, like inverted drains, spouting their smoke into the oily taste of the air. And over all the half-daze of dream, the hanging haze, mist, soot and steam, the smell of gas, boiled fish and washing.

Then slowly I grew attuned to this special climate. Through the murk I heard chickens, children and the chatter of women. I realized, in fact, that this was no desert, but a world of homes, a place alive and busy. For the valley hummed with work; looms buzzed and rumbled, furnaces roared, lathes squealed and shunting engines piped and trumpeted, blowing bright bubbles of steam into the sky. The day warmed up, the heavy air lightened from grey to gold.

It was at this moment that I saw my first legitimate sign of spring, such a sign, perhaps, as one would see nowhere else, but genuine as a cuckoo. In a long damp street, whose sooty walls had transformed it into a deep channel of darkness, a row of lamps flared suddenly, like yellow crocuses, their gas jets lit and bubbling. And standing alternately between them, of the same height and colour, was an avenue of trees, stunted, black-stemmed and lopped, but likewise alight with jets of sharp green leaves. With such shadowy symbols to cling to, my eyes began to focus, and then at last I saw Slagtown in its own spring light.

All the next day I wandered about, and the town's own carbon copy of itself unrolled before me. I toiled up and down hills, under a lattice of trolley wires, past innumerable co-op shops, and mission halls full of throaty singing. I walked a hundred streets of square black houses, past stained-glass doors, and doorsteps washed bright yellow. Through a hundred front windows I saw the broad leaf of the perennial aspidistra (that household ikon of pagan green). Through a hundred others I saw high teas laid out upon their tables, a ritual of sausage, lettuce and hot meat pies. And in the back streets by the station I saw the markets piled with the crated fruits of springs of other lands: South African grapes, Italian peas, Canary tomatoes, Dutch cucumbers, azaleas, wallflowers and potted tulips – the death-spoils of winter, and all for Slagtown.

But that was not everything. On my way about, of course, I met some people. The season shone through them too.

These were not faces I had seen before. They were northern faces, craggy, more friendly than most, the faces of craftsmen, spinners, weavers. Little men with cloth caps and short black pipes, with sulphurous skins, bird-blue eyes, and a manner of talking that was a joy to listen to. I saw handsome girls, in brilliant coats and scarves, crowding, with airs of carnival, the buses outside the Cloth Hall. I saw old women, in knitted shawls, debating, through the plate-glass windows of a dress shop, the styles of the Easter brides on show within. And two boys in the street, dithering with bat and ball, while a third painted wickets on the gasworks wall. Spring, willy-nilly, was here.

And there was more to prove it. From the stir and mass of the milling town you could break off a short scene, chew it, and taste most readily the tang in the air.

An old man with short legs and a scarlet waistcoat, cocky as a robin, led his granddaughter to a piece of waste ground behind the mill. He was finished with the mill for good; he and the child carried a kite between them; it was playtime now forever.

'Aye, it's been a grand winter, son,' he said. 'Real grand. Easy on the bones. And spring's early. Me 'ens are laying like mad.'

And he gave the kite to the girl and she ran off with it on her red legs and it rose with a swoop into the yellow air and he watched it.

A carrot-haired woman in a bun-shop took twopence from a tobacco tin to buy a bottle of vinegar.

'Me old man's been cutting his lettuce,' she said, 'and I'm going to make us a salad. Gave me three 'a'pence for the vinegar. But that'll never be enough – as I told him.'

A young blond innkeeper, home from the navy, looked over the bar and said in a strangled voice:

'Slagtown! Awful place. They bin and changed all the bus stops. I – I can't bear it.'

The barmaid looked at him from brown eyes smothered with love.

'It'll be all reet, Jim,' she said softly. 'It'll be all reet . . .'

A bunch of brushed youths, in belted mackintoshes, stood outside the cinema, and their talk mingled sport with fancy.

'Why are all the females around 'ere such whoppers?' asked one. 'They'd make a reet good football team.'

'Aye, they would that,' said another, and added sadly, 'but I wouldn't mind being the football . . .'

A stiff-backed weaver was walking beside me up a long steep road.

'I like these 'ills,' he said warmly. 'I reckon they're real luvly. Can't do wi' level country, lad. I tried it once. Couldn't get a bit o' breath. I was yawn, yawn, yawn, all the time. But I loves the 'ills. 'Specially in April. They freshens you up like a filbert . . .'

Then out in that no-man's-land, past the end of the trolley buses, where the stone road rises to sheep walls and little blackened farms, I found Jasper, aged seventy-two. We were raised to the tops of the valley chimneys, above the steam clouds, looking down on the slag heaps, the starch-blue stagnant pools, the sweating railways and custard-thick canals.

Jasper was shovelling soil out of a bank into four buckets. He wanted it for his garden. As soon as I spoke to him I knew he was no ordinary man.

'I've the longest memory in the valley,' he said. 'And I see the future of the world.'

'Tell me the future,' I asked.

Jasper grew close, and struck his hands together. He grinned grimly, and roared like a preacher, in full rich periods beautifully timed and chanted.

'I'm old,' he said, 'and I thank God I'm getting out of it! Greed! It'll reduce this world to ashes. What with supersonical waves and silent sound – we could be standing here, lad, and they'd knock us down like mice.'

He talked for two hours, with the mills thumping in the valley and the sparrows screaming around his head. Then, suddenly, the spring hit him, too, poor Jasper, and he clapped his hand to his mouth with a cry of anguish.

'What's the matter?' I asked.

'It's me gums, lad,' he said. 'The worst thing I ever did. Had 'em opened up top and bottom. Thirty-eight X-rays – thirty top and four deep – wi' cockaine injections too numerous to mention. But they 'as me beat. The spring air's cruel to 'em – makes 'em jump and jangle. I could keep you talking all day. But it's me gums. They've gone bitter. Now I'll 'ave to take 'em 'ome and warm 'em. Besides –' and he loaded a barrow with his buckets of earth '– I've got to catch this weather with me taters.'

So I left Jasper and climbed up on the moor above the chemical works. It would soon be time to take the train and return again to the south. What had I gathered from this steamy cauldron, these endless, similar valleys of clotted streams, stone mills, sharp men, jaunty girls, and graves with rare, archaic names? Well, it was spring; bitter, brave, submerged – but irresistible.

I sat on a rock and looked for the last time on Slagtown. The haze had not passed, but was still dream-like, almost Chinese. Sounds rose; the rattle of trucks, bark of dogs, cry of children and flutter of homing pigeons. The sun rolled through the steaming air as white and slippery as a ball of mercury. But it was Saturday afternoon, and there was a smell of green and a feel of holiday. I heard a brass band tuning up. Shouts came from an invisible sports field. Men were scratching hard, like hares, in small black gardens; while boys and girls sailed forth on shining bikes.

It was not what I expected; but as I sat there, the picture fell into place before me, genuine and vivid. Slagtown had met the season full tilt, and in its own way.

Meanwhile, on the moors above, among the raw dark rocks, the sheep were dropping their dusty lambs. And out of the black sour grass skylarks went spinning, singing into the clouds.

Conversations in The Sun

No artificial fertilizers of wireless or television ever interfered with its scrubby growth. Hard- or soft-rooted, the talk lived or withered under the beer's celestial dew.

Charlie Moss, eighty-six, dipped his whiskers in it, then blew them out like wings. 'I ain't seen thee since the spring of the year, charming the birds 'long the edge of the wood.'

That would do for a start; he was always a bit fancy. He lived alone and acknowledged no one. He handed round walnuts he'd grown himself and giggled, for they were all of them rotten.

The Sun public house stands in a steep western valley, has a horse-trough and a perpetual spring of sweet water. Its cellars inside are full of local-brewed beers that keep the same temperature, winter and summer. The building dates back to the sixteenth century but looks as old as the valley itself, from whose gaping hillsides its stones and tiles were all originally ripped.

Mr Moss continued to giggle in his corner. There were also present Albert Hawkes and the landlady.

'I was born in a pub and got married in jail,' she said suddenly. 'What you think you're doing?' Nobody was doing anything much, but Mrs Uley liked this announcement. She was the daughter, in fact, of a Gloucester innkeeper, and had married a warder from Bristol Prison – enough to claim special knowledge of both beer and the law, and to give her the whip hand over her customers.

'. . . And then I got me orders to blow me whistle because the peace had been declared.' Mr Hawkes, the egg-seller, was back in the Canada of 1918, remembering no other time since then. He spoke in a Cotswold-Canadian accent, was eighty-four, and wore a black homburg hat. 'Ah called to the engineers to give me more air and watched the gauge slowly comin' up. Then ah went to me whistle – it was off a big lake steamer an' you could hear it twelve miles away – and ah pulled on the rope, an' tied it round a stanchion, an' kep' it blowin' fer twenny-four hours.'

Bertie Bates came in with a goldfish bowl, accompanied by Wally Silver, the farmer.

'Fill 'er up,' said Bates, slamming the bowl on the bar. 'She'll 'old at least a gallon.'

'Hallo, me darlins,' roared Mr Silver. 'Lord, ain't I glad to see you! Listen. Listen 'ere . . . I got summat to tell ya. Now don't you say nothin'. Listen . . .'

'It tipped with rain while I was comin' up,' Bates said. 'I spilt that there fish in the pond.'

'Listen, me dear. Bide quiet an' listen. Listen what I goin' to say . . .'

'I still got me budgies. They half drive me crazy. They kick up 'ell with the radio on.'

'Listen,' begged Silver, whirling his arms about. 'Last night I didn't half scream. There was all them courtin' couples up in the quarry. Listen what I was going to tell ya . . . I come up quiet. I was mounted on rubber.' He showed the heels of his plimsoll shoes. 'Well, I caught 'em proper. I bursted out laughin'. That did it. Lord, I died.'

He'd retired from his farming and moved into a cottage, and was bright-eyed and much on the loose.

'See this straw 'at? Cost me seven and sixpence. Oh, yes.' He yelped. 'Ain't I wunnerful? I be have three young ladies to tea today. Served 'em me £30 tea-set, with salmon.'

''E could drink like a goldfish, too,' said Bates. 'Tich Williams – you remember 'im? One night 'e got drunk, we tied a foal to 'is bike. "Drat you! Get away! Stop followin' I!" Up the road 'e went, zigzag . . .'

'All the Lords and Ladies of Stroud,' cried Silver. 'They be all a-comin' to see me. They're wantin' to put me on the telephone. I can 'andle government to perfection.'

What water had he got in his fine new cottage, which some said was falling down?

'Why, the beautiful main-water what the Lord put on ten thousand year ago, better by far of high degree than that council drizzle from Stroud.'

The beer on the bar was now standing in regiments, rough brown, the colour of beechnuts. Quoits were flying about the room, and Mrs Uley was getting the spikes. In came the Doons, short father, tall son, as they did every night of the year. Dad was powerful as a donkey-engine, the son fair, loose-limbed and handsome. He had round eager eyes and adored his father. They were both of them black with soot.

'Evenin' all,' they said in chorus. 'Chock us a Cotswold, missus.'

'Badgers,' said Dad, 'is the cleanest animal there is. They live in deep. They got proper 'ouses.'

'They got proper 'ouses,' echoed the son. 'True as I'm standing 'ere. Front room, bedroom, nursery, kitchen, top floor and bottom floor!'

'Can't 'unt 'em with dogs though. Dogs is just helpless. They'll scratch 'is parts right off.'

'Why 'unt 'em at all then? They bin takin' yer chickens?'

'They'd have to be 'ard put to it to take a chicken. They'd 'ave to be 'ard put to it, you. They'll take blackberries, now; they like blackberries, you. But they wouldn't take a chicken. They like grubs an' slugs an' beetles an' that. If they finds a bees' nest, they'll take that'n, too . . .'

'Dad; he says why trap 'em, then?'

'For the skin an' the fat. Worth a lot that is, you know. They makes what's-its, what-d'you-call-'ems, shaving brushes with the 'airs. Worth a lot that is, the fur. And they 'as all that fat just unner the skin. Shift anything that will, you. Just rub it across the back of yer 'and an' it'll come right out through the palm. Rub it on yer chest an' it'll go right through. Shift anything, that will, you.'

'It'll go through steel,' said Gerry, the son. 'Shift anything, badger fat. Used to catch 'em early mornings, didn't we, dad? Boil 'em in a gurt iron copper. Fat used to sweat right through the copper an' come out the other side. Very good for rheumatism. Go through anything. Shift anything that will, you.'

Father Doon, who was now the gasworks' stoker, had once been a prodigious poacher.

'Few young 'uns knows how to trap a rabbit. Couldn't set a long net for their lives. I reckon young Ayres was the last one I learned. Nearly got shot in the back fer me trouble.'

'Remember when you went out shootin' rabbits and shot that old mule instead?'

'Well, they got the same ears,' said Dad.

It was bottled beer now, and a game of darts, but the older men wouldn't play.

'Darts?' said Bates. 'Me and 'im were champions. Both lost it, just like that. One night I got six treble-twennies in a row. Next day I couldn't do nothing.'

'Same with me,' said Doon. 'Used to play for the League. Can't get nothing no more. Picked up a stone to throw at a bird one day. Thought me arm 'ad come right off.'

'Old men can't do it. Nor the married 'uns. They get the shakes an' then they've 'ad it. Like Sid, from the works, with all them daughters. He was in bed one night, one of his girls came 'ome, switched the radio on full wallop. He shouted turn it off. The wife turned it off. Another daughter came in, switched it on again. Father got up, fetched his twelve-bore gun, walked down to the kitchen, shot the wireless to pieces and made a bloody great 'ole in the wall.'

'That milk-'orse I 'ad; 'e used to like music. Martial music particular. A dismal beast, but if 'e 'eard a band playing 'e'd step out like a warrior.'

'Funny, that. Like this Bedford of mine. I likes to sing when I'm driving. Well, that engine changes tune just when I wan' it to – he can follow anything.'

Father Doon's soot-black face had changed with the beer, washed clean round the lips.

'I'm back stokin', y'know. It's no good, I just love it. Can't keep away from it somehow.'

'The Stokers of 'Ell they call 'em,' said the son. 'You should see the togs they wear. Top 'ats with the lids bobbin' up and down, odd boots, a slipper, a clog. The fire draws the nails right out of their uppers, true as I'm standing 'ere.'

'I must of read 'undreds and thousands of books down there. Ain't much to do between stoking. I was readin' one night, young Gerry was with me. He was starin' around, all nervous. Suddenly he says, "What's that, dad?" I could see 'is eyes poppin' out. I says, "Them's the spirits of the dead what 'ave died on the job. Just keep quiet, an' don't say nothin'." There's this boiler, see, up the end of the passage, and drifts of steam come dancing along. Then the draught might change, and the steam hangs still, 'alf up in the air, a-watchin' you.'

'Aye,' said Gerry, 'and wi' a gurt cowl on top. Horrible, an' that's the truth.'

'There's hundreds of crickets runnin' up an' down them boilers. An' rats – but I don't pay attention. One night young Gerry brought me down me supper and started shootin' the crickets with a pistol. He was still a-shootin' of 'em at four o'clock in the mornin'. Had to walk back to Whiteshill on his own.'

'Whiteshill were a shade different then,' said Gerry. 'We 'ad it all sewed up. Any outside chaps come a-courtin' our girls 'ad to pay us a gallon of beer. None of the police never came near us. Dad once threw a chap down the quarry.'

Father Doon displayed his battered right fist with its swollen, coagulated muscles.

'Them's the marks of 'is teeth. He were beatin' my pal. Course they've shut a lot of the pubs.'

'I was born in a pub and got married in jail. Now come on the lot of you!'

Men bowed, bowed down, and put on their cycle-clips. Pockets were loaded with bottles . . .

> *(It was early one morning at the break of the day,*
> *The cocks were a-crowing, the Farmer did say:*
> *'Come rise my good fellows, come rise with a will,*
> *Your horses want something their bellies to fill . . .')*

'See you tomorrow then. Shan't change, of course. Though it ain't that I 'aven't got it.'

> *(Then seven o'clock comes and to breakfast we meet*
> *Of pork, bread and mutton so merrily eat,*
> *With a piece in our pocket away then we go,*
> *We're all jolly fellows that follow the plough . . .)*

'Can't get no sleep. It's them damn mice a-gnawing.'
'Give 'em Rodine – that'll croak 'em.'

> *(Our master come to us and this he did say:*
> *'What have you been doing all this long day?*
> *You've not ploughed your acre I swear and I vow*
> *You're damn idle fellows that follow the plough . . .')*

'Come on, Bert – put a sock in it.'

Mr Moss and Mr Hawkes followed their dogs through the door. The valley was dark outside.

'Listen,' said Mr Silver. 'Listen what I goin' to say . . . I'll give you a half-crown to take me 'ome . . .'

The Last Ten Years

A decade in the country can slip down the gullet with the deceptive smoothness of an oyster. Yet the last ten years have marked rural life more than anything done to it for centuries.

Ten years ago my home village in the Cotswolds was very much like it had been in my childhood.

In 1954 we had a noisy village school (doubling as a village hall), a busy communal life, a noticeable absence of motor cars and a mildly dazed vicar-in-residence. On late spring evenings, while the men forked their gardens, their wives trumpeted 'Jerusalem' from the schoolroom. There were regular dances for the young (to ominous cries of 'yeah! yeah! yeah!'), whist drives and occasional 'socials'.

Then, almost stealthily, the changes began. The school was closed, and by the same stroke we lost our village hall. The playtime voices were stilled, the dances and meetings stopped and the school auctioned off as a desirable property. So the children lost, as did the rest of us, our village centre, and all were driven back upon less-shared diversions.

The once free-ranging children are now ferried to the town schools in the mornings then back in their sealed buses to family television in the evening. Footpaths grow over where folk have the lack of will to tread, and with the death of the rabbit, jungles sprawl on the commons. The great beechwoods and fields, once immemorially open to all, are slowly being boarded and barbed-wired by the farmer.

As for the farmer himself – suddenly he realizes that he is one of the lords of life. With new machinery and techniques, he commands his worlds, buys up his neighbours, burns his stubble and hedges, batteries his hens, concentrates his pigs and yields the once sacred act of harvesting to the travelling 'contractor'.

Money, mobility, the city-financier's slide-rule, the bulldozer, changes of habit and faith, the big battalions of the brewery and the motor car industries – all these in the last decade have redesigned the landscape and country life. Many village pubs have been closed and most of the survivors degutted and relined with false beams and Costa Brava ironwork. Most local breweries have disappeared together with their happily multi-flavoured beers, to be replaced by the gaseous hiss of keg bitter which now blankets the lands.

Some things have not changed, have even taken on stronger emphases and value: the care of gardens, wine-making and gossip, the annual rain-drenched fête and flower show. Though most elm trees, alas, are dead or dying, there is still that incomparable light falling on the pastoral scene, streams jumping with fish, woods full of unpackaged birds and at night the soft pad of the badger.

Chelsea Bun

When my mother sensed that the time had come for me to leave home, she suggested, halfway between a giggle and a sigh, that I might do worse than go and live in Chelsea. She was a country girl, had never strayed far from her roots, but to her, a great reader of romantic novelettes, Chelsea was a place of high-tone fantasy, of bearded genius, swooning beauties, and garlanded studios over-hanging the river.

I'd only thought of Chelsea as a football team and a currant bun, but I took Mother at her word, believing I was carrying out some secret instruction, and when I set out to see the world I settled in Chelsea towards the end of the war, and have lived here, on and off, ever since.

I began with a bedsit in Markham Square, the top-floor window commanding a history of time. My friend and landlord was the Keeper of the Public Records Office, a cultured and careful man, who, in order to save fuel, went to bed at sundown and read Proust by the light of a saucerful of glow-worms sent up from the country in jam jars.

Chelsea, then, had no cars, few people, and vast emptying skies enlivened only by steam from Battersea Power Station. The King's Road had curled old ladies selling needles and thread, work-men's cafés serving kipper-teas for a shilling; upside-down butcher's shops, with meat hanging under the counter; and dairies with china eggs and cardboard cows decorating otherwise empty shelves.

I don't suppose Chelsea differed, in this regard, from any-where else at the time, but it had that distinguishing presence my mother's instinct had promised, and Markham Square certainly was a compact little enclave of oddities, a fringe gathering of painters, poets and muses.

Halfway through the morning I'd see Dylan Thomas, like a plump, furry little mole, pop up from his basement opposite and go padding off to the pub. If we met in the street we didn't speak, but nodded. I was teetotal in those days, and certain lines were drawn. Two doors to my left lived the incomparable James Cameron, and we used to play the violin and guitar together. Not well; but those were days of no discos and little public entertainment, and sometimes we hired an old pony-trap and toured the streets in a selfless attempt to enrapture the populace.

Further up, Elizabeth Smart, her face emblazoned with light, mothered the happy brood of George Barker's children; while across the square, issuing nervously from some mysterious recess of his own, the poet Paul Potts, a tall, stooping figure, stumbled his way to the shops. He caused me no offence, but thinking there were too many poets around, I took a shot at him one day with an airgun. The pellet hit him in the foot, he leapt in the air, turned round and berated some innocent old woman behind him, and left immediately for the Hebrides.

In Markham Square I saw the last days of the war, with German bombers dropping cascades of coloured lights, Chelsea never looking more beautiful, all-night parties in Victorian coal-holes, and sunken cheeks in the morning. Chelsea grew increasingly deserted. One bright August evening I stood in the middle of the King's Road and shot an arrow from The Markham Arms to the old Town Hall. It bounced unhindered up the empty street. Only a stray dog stepped out of the way.

My quiver empty, my arrows spent, I moved into Edna O'Brien's house in Carlyle Square – though unhappily our habitation did not coincide. It was the late forties, early fifties. The last all clear had sounded. People returned to their abandoned houses. Chelsea took a long deep breath and prepared for pleasure, and began to put on paint like a debutante. Women shrugged off their square-rigged shoulders and military suits and became beribboned and cuddly again. A bachelor then, I was occasionally visited by girls in loose Hungarian blouses. While from downstairs in the basement one heard slaps, shrieks of laughter, and the padding of bare feet on the floorboards. Sex had never seemed more carefree or funnier.

From the winter grey of war, Chelsea was turning its expectant face towards that pleasure dome it so hoped to become. But in those early fifties, before the Conrans and the Quants had slapped down their manorial rights on the place, there still remained remnants of that elegant village Mother had imagined Chelsea to be – T. S. Eliot, in clerical hat and dark mackintosh, pushing John Hayward round the streets in his wheelchair, Eliot slightly bent and listening to Hayward's incessant chatter as though eloquence was the vehicle's chief propellant. Then Sir Alfred Munnings, in hacking jacket and jodhpurs, striking the railings with his riding crop; Epstein hurrying from his studio showered in sky-blue clay; Edith Sitwell walking in reverie . . . Her brother, Sir Osbert, lived a few doors away, a man of deceptively livid appearance, even when some children and I, one bonfire night, put a flaming rocket through his first-floor window and burnt a hole in his Elizabethan arras.

All gone now, that lot. Even the long-legged schoolgirl who used to deliver my newspapers on rollerskates and was later to marry a lord. I married too, and moved to Elm Park Gardens, several streets away.

This three-sided square of kipper-coloured houses was stuffed then with the families from the bombed East End. The last time, perhaps, for such a select Chelsea garden to ring with the jungle-cries of the scab-kneed poor. No 'Simons', 'Samanthas' or 'Clarissas', yet, but 'Sids' and 'Berts' and 'Brendas'. The boys, scrub-haired and nutty-headed, sons of the coastal marauders of western Europe, having drifted upriver on tides of generations; and their sisters, sharp-eyed, squinting, sly and seductive: 'You a hundred yet, Mr Lee?'

All day the boys played cricket in the road, and the girls chalked square games as old as Byzantium. Or stood on their heads in the garden in squealing rows of stalky thighs and blooming knickers.

Mid-fifties, pre-television, perhaps never again in Chelsea would families live out of doors on summer evenings, children playing, mothers gossiping on doorsteps, chewing hard-peas and shrieking with laughter, babies rocking, dogs barking, cats slinking, pigeons panicking, while short bantam husbands, settling their caps and mufflers, trotted away down to their pubs.

Among this rollicking community I was privileged to rent a small flat in a house owned by the Chelsea Housing Improvement Society, a discreet little charity devoted to preserving the past and to which my slender cultural pretensions endowed me. Next door a young painter, of some renown and promise, lived with a wife of whom he was coldly and clinically jealous. He kept her locked up in the basement, and took her out twice a day to the gardens, and told her to run up and down. This done, he took her home and locked her up again. She turned out to be a better painter than he was.

Before the coming of the sterilized wine bars and the brewer's boardroom of extravaganzas, Chelsea offered a treasury of little rusticated pubs – The Potter, The Markham Arms, The Eight Bells, The Cadogan, The Roebuck, The Man in the Moon, and Finch's. The Eight Bells had Trog with his band of Trad Jazz upstairs, but otherwise into the sixties most of our pubs had scrubbed institutional tables and benches, with Battersea mums and dads drinking their twinkling stout in happy silence and swinging their short legs a foot from the floor.

Towards the mid-sixties the tribal cries of the East End kids were silenced, they and their families swept up into the council's new filing boxes down World's End way. We were not to hear their lively calls again. The dumb, parked motor car began to occupy their chalked games and scuffed playgrounds, and with them a new breed of money.

In Chelsea, especially, money and the inchoate days of returning peace created a space to be filled with pantomime, plumage, sensation, invention and show. There was a more opulent tribalism now which, reacting against the uniformity of war, rejected, then reflected, in increasingly extreme forms, more frenetic group uniformities.

Teds, skinheads, boys in braces and bovver boots, Mods and Rockers, a pretty fluttering of miniskirted girls, Twiggy models like boys, a sweep of Samanthas in pantaloons from the hunting shires, then more lately the grotesqueries of Punk. Chelsea Punk, where it was fathered, suggested revolution, and at the beginning perhaps it was; but now it seems to conform to its own diktat as regimentally as all the others. At first one could but applaud these cartoons of protest – the secret zips and leg-straps, pierced ears and noses, electrified hair and hints of self-flagellation.

Punk – commercialized and domesticated – is now just another fragment of Chelsea graffiti for which we can still feel some declining affection. But at least it let in the girls, so they could walk hand in hand with their men, each stamped black as Lucifer in their chains.

We'd seen all this expanding, in spurts of ebullience, from their drab, end-of-the-war beginnings to their kaleidoscopic present, from the day when Quentin Crisp first stepped through pools of fastidious disapproval along pavements now blocked by his unremarked imitations.

Over the years we've watched Chelsea emerge from its quiet, cultured chrysalis to the diamond-dotted butterfly it has now become. It has passed through its stages of transformation, from greenery-yallery to Reject-Habitatory, meat pie and mash to Pizza Express, from beans with everything to jeans with everything, second-hand bookshops replaced by little-rich-girl boutiques customarily named 'Ibiza' or 'Shangri-La'.

Chelsea is rich now, one of the prime oil-gushers of London, its fame and fantasies lubricated worldwide by fashion-sheets, films and the jet plane. The old pubs have been deloused, degutted, carpeted and tinselled, their names the only remnant of what they once were, like the names of old towns since violated.

Almost permanently scaffolded, Chelsea still has some handsome old houses whose value increases three times a day – inhabited by handsome couples, tall, tanned and double colour-spread, with permanently scaffolded marriages.

A place still almost completely unchanged since its founding, by

Whistler and friends a century ago, is the Chelsea Arts Club towards the north end of Old Church Street. A small door in a plain wall opens into something only Chelsea could offer, a charming little house of taste and antiquity – reading-rooms, billiard-rooms, bedrooms and dining-rooms all hanging with excellent pictures of the founding time. And beyond that all a walled garden past belief: trees, lawns, fountains and a resident tortoise.

When I first joined the Arts Club, in the late 1940s, membership was almost entirely confined to artists, their models and mistresses, their varnishers, picture-framers and agents. It was leisured and usually half-empty. Now the Arts Club has suddenly become The Place To Be, and almost any evening you'll see a coloured crowd pouring through the small plain door like bees drawn into a hole – dark-suited workers, bright striped drones, royal-jelly-fed beauty queens. The past and the present are preserved in the Club, from white-whiskered artists to sugar-fringed models.

Meanwhile, up and down Old Church Street wander the tourists, maps in hand like Minoan clay tablets, asking: 'Vich vay, pliss – the Chelsea Road, yes? The King's Road, pliss?'

I love Chelsea – after all, it's my second home – but for all its slick shops and restaurants, licensed to print T-shirts and money, it has largely become a parody of what it imagined itself to be, a place to which people travel great distances to find themselves taking photographs of each other, an arena almost entirely filled with spectators.

The Shining Severn

When I was a child, so young that I hardly knew what water was, I remember lying on my belly on a Cotswold hill, surrounded by grasshoppers and cardinal butterflies, and gazing through the long grass at the Gloucester plain below. The plain had a great shining piece of sky in it, a curving, glittering sheet of sky above which blue mountains rose like the landscape of heaven.

I was lying on a hill above Stroud, and this is the view I saw, and the curving piece of sky I was looking at was the shining river of the west – the Severn.

The Severn is the second largest river in Britain. It curves in a great shining loop through five western counties, and for ages has been the frontier river separating the hill tribes of Wales from the successive invaders of England. Let us go down to the hills of Wales, to the fountainhead of this river, and follow its course to the sea.

The Severn rises in Plynlimon mountain, a few miles from the sea near Aberystwyth. Plynlimon is a great rising ground of rivers. At least four well up from its mossy pools and take their separate courses. The Rheidol and Ystwyth have brisk brief lives, scampering straight to the nearby sea. The Wye runs south, winding through lovely wooded valleys to its mouth at Chepstow. But the Severn turns its back on the ocean altogether and aims straight for the heart of middle England, giving birth to abbeys, cathedrals, cities, and travelling two hundred headstrong miles before its life is done.

This is the young Severn near its source, slipping, bouncing and bubbling down little green gorges whose banks are stuffed with lead mines and ringed by ancient cairns. So the river would have appeared in its early days to the buzzards and hawks that fly these lonely skies. Over two thousand feet above the sea, there is nothing else to watch its tumbling source, but sheep, foxes, rabbits and wild ponies. Here the Severn is light and fast and free, tumbling in little waterfalls and racing round stones. These are its miles of infancy and carelessness. It runs its capricious course in quick loops westward, and is hardly aware of being a river at all, until it enters Llanidloes, the first township on its banks.

At Llanidloes the sparkling Plynlimon stream is first proved a river and a pathfinder. Here the road and the railway join the river to use the valley it has given them. Here also it is joined and strengthened by a tributary, who also rose in Plynlimon. Thus grown and broadened, but not yet sobered, the Severn ambles northeast to Caersws, the site of a Roman outpost which, when it was first set up here, still in the heart of Wales, must have seemed to the garrison a camp on the edge of the world.

All rivers are neutral. They will act as a defensive moat to the defender, or just as easily turn traitor and lead the invader through the hill passes just as the Severn led the Romans to Caersws. No wonder they are feared and worshipped. They are barriers to men and protectors. Life grows from them as from a stalk. At Newtown the Severn makes a little casual arm, but within the curve of this arm the men of Newtown founded their fortress.

Here at Newtown a canal appears – the Shropshire Union Canal, walking staidly by the ambling river and censoriously cutting out the bends. But the Severn is still the ancient guide, cutting through the round rough hill and pointing the way in and out of Wales. This is still the best and only way, and where the river goes the road, canal and railway all closely follow.

The riverway past Welshpool now is northward, wild and green. The banks are lined with rich but shaggy pastures. Ash, oak, birch and willow hang over the banks. In this quiet landscape you will see white owls, and hear the curlew and the sandpiper. Quiet as this landscape may seem now, the river was once the heart of border strife and savagery. The villages are built on the layers of ashes of many burnings. The hills and meadows are scarred with ancient battles. Here in 894, in this field near Buttington Bridge, King Alfred, helped by the men of Powys, slaughtered an invasion of the Danes and choked the river with their corpses.

After Shrewsbury the Severn changes course and turns south-west. It is still an erratic and impetuous river, winding, shallowing and scampering over rapids, but it is entering into some of its loveliest country. The fields hereabout belonged once to Squire Mytton, the beloved Shropshire eccentric who married a mermaid he fished out of the river, and who cured his hiccoughs by setting fire to the tail of his nightshirt.

Further on, the meadows are full of ghosts, for here is the site of the Roman Uriconium, still littered with mounds under the grass. Uriconium was another of those towns fathered by the river, and was one of the last on the Welsh frontier. Poised on the barbarous edge of the known world, Uriconium was a fair city of fine buildings, with basilica, public baths, villas, temples. It was burned at last by the West Saxons, and for over a thousand years sheep grazed above the smoke-blackened bones of the victims of that pillage.

The Severn now is the heart of Shropshire; it runs singing through rich and dramatic country. To the south, Wenlock Edge lifts its thick leaf-tufted skyline to seethe and blow in the westward winds. To the north, like an aged and sprouting pyramid, stands the Wrekin, eerie of name and drenched with blood and memories. Like Breidden Hill, the Wrekin is another fortress height to which the men of the river withdrew in times of trouble. Peaked with tumuli and encampments, it is heavy with legend and rich with macabre names such as the Raven's Bowl and the Gates of Heaven and Hell.

This of course is Housman's country. The hills, trees, winds, men and battle, the ghosts of blood in the Severn water – all of these moved him to a moment of intense poignancy in his ballads. Man's tragedy hereabouts was no doubt more savage, less fragile; but you cannot look at Wenlock now without remembering Housman's still and singing voice.

Leaving Wenlock and the woods of the Wrekin, past Buildwas Abbey and the landslip where, two hundred years ago, the bed of the river is supposed to have burst fifty feet into the air, changing the river's course, the Severn is suddenly pulled tight into a gorge and the landscape darkens. For here, out of the spacious green of Buildwas, a curious outcrop of the Black Country emerges. All the names in the valley – Coalbrookdale, Ironbridge, Coalport – reflect the change. Industry has punched this valley black. The river is ragged and soiled. There are coal pits, slag heaps, steel foundries. The rocks of the valley are full of coal and iron.

Ironbridge takes its name, simply enough, from the bridge of iron which spans the river here. It was the first bridge of this kind ever cast in the world. Over 150 years old, with a span of one hundred feet, it possesses today a slight, almost Chinese charm. The engineer Wilkinson, who built this bridge, also built a cast-iron barge here, and launched it, in 1780, amidst universal doubt and derision. To the local farmers it was a gigantic folly, like building a ploughshare of paper. But the iron craft floated, and Wilkinson wrote: 'and so I convinced the unbelievers, who were 999 to the thousand'.

From Coalport the Severn turns south at last, shakes off its industrial dust, and takes on again an air of gracious elegance. This is a turning point in the life and quality of the river. The next town is Bridgnorth, a pleasant slumberous town with an old stone bridge and red sandstone cliffs above it. On southward through the thick Wyre Forest, past Bewdley, once a famous centre for barge traffic, now decayed and tranquil, to Stourport, where a canal comes in and the Stour adds its waters to the main river.

The Severn now is broad, mature and navigable. It has come of age. From its tumbling, racing headquarters, it has grown smooth, deep and slow – a place for meditation. It is said that this stretch of the Severn once had more religious foundations than anywhere else in Britain. Near this island, for instance, there is a hermitage in the rocky bank said to be capably of holding a hundred holy men. There are others, too, scattered along the banks. But this holy valley has not been without its times of shock and turbulence. The inhabitants of Worcester city twice crowded for refuge upon this small island – once for protection against the Danes, and once in terror of the Plague.

Three miles south of Bevere Island rises the redstone cathedral of the river's first city – Worcester. It stands on steep banks of rock, facing west to the Malvern Hills (which Byron, as a boy, first saw with rapture, a foretaste of the grape-blue hills of Greece). The river, leaving Worcester, runs parallel with the Malvern range, and at little Upton-upon-Severn reveals itself as a full-grown river of ships in the existence of these docks. A few miles more, at Tewkesbury, there is another meeting of the waters, as the Avon comes in from the east, mixing the dust of Shakespeare's town in the roar of the tumbling water.

Tewkesbury's abbey is one of the finest in England. This great golden-coloured tower, booming with bells, could well be a grass-grown ruin like all the others, if it had not been for the townsfolk of Tewkesbury, who bought it from Henry VIII, at the time of the dissolution, for £550. And what a bargain they had of it.

At Tewkesbury the Severn first smells the sea, faint tremors of tides run up towards the weir, and there is traffic on the river dropping down to Gloucester. Gloucester is a city older than memory. In its time it has had many names. The Iberians called it Caer Glow, or beautiful city. In Roman days its name was Glevum – which may have come from Gle-Avon, or shining river. The Romans held it until the sixth century as a stronghold against river pirates. Since then it has been a seat of parliament and of kings. It was a besieged fortress during the parliamentary wars, and martyrs have been burned in its streets. And all its crowded life and history have sprung from the river, because it held the gateway to the wilds of Wales and the estuary to the sea.

Now, as the river opens in broad sweeps past the great orchards of Minsterworth and Epney, it flushes daily with the currents of the sea. Sea fish and river fish mingle together, and wild geese inhabit the meadows and sandbanks. The Severn is coming back to its home in the sea, and it has come back to my home also, to the point where I first saw it. It is a major river by now, a shining river of light by day, and at evening, when the sun drops into the hills of Wales, a river of blood.

This stretch of the Severn, from Sharpness to Gloucester, is the part I know best. My grandfather used to spear eels with a trident here. Playmates used to flop off the banks like frogs. And on Good Friday, every year, in the time of the spring equinox, we would gather here to watch the Bore. The spring Bore is the most dramatic event on the river, and is seen at its best where the river narrows above Frampton. As the high-peaked tide thrusts up from the sea it is piled like a heaped wave by the narrowing banks. As it comes, you hear it roaring far away, then there it is, boiling, seething, sweeping round the bends, frothing high at the banks, and tossing boats high.

To the novice, afloat, it can be death. But the old fishermen and bargemen of the river can ride it like a wild horse for miles upstream. Bargemen used to follow it and make it pull them up to Gloucester, taking the orchards of Minsterworth in one sweep of their eighteen-foot oars. The Bore divides and weakens when it hits Gloucester Island, but nervous tremors of it will run up as far as Tewkesbury to pile up and die against the weir.

The days of the great river bargemen are over now, for meek canals have cancelled the Severn's tides and curves. At Upper Framilode a canal runs up to the woollen mills of Stroud, and at Sharpness the Berkeley Canal takes over from the sweeping river and runs in a straight line to Gloucester. To the docks of Sharpness ocean ships can come, unloading onto the barges their cargoes from the Baltic and the Indies. Here the Severn broadens fast, half-sea, half-river. The sandbanks grow large, and the estuary appears.

At Beachley Point the Wye comes wandering in, having run its own course from Plynlimon; and the Severn, reunited with its brother, is reunited also with its native soil of Wales. After Beachley Point the Severn opens and swells like the climax of a symphony. Here, beneath the rocky bed, the railway tunnel runs into Newport – the last terrestrial crossing. From now on you cross by boat or not at all. For the river has come of age. No more punts, weirs, locks, eel-spears and wading cattle. South is the port of Bristol. North are the black valleys of the Rhondda and Cardiff, the great port of colliers. The small unnoticed stream which bubbled from the mossy pools of Plynlimon has grown to this breadth of water, it has run its course, it has given life to a chain of towns and cities, and now the ports on its banks can barely see each other, lighthouses wink in midstream, and great ships are specks on its waters.

The Severn is a river no longer. The Severn has become the sea.

Summer

Summertime

You can sometimes tell it almost before waking up by its warm green breath on the eyelids. Then rich and sudden as a lucky gamble, hoped for but hardly expected, the flowered days come, a three-ringed circus, and everything happens at once. Almost overnight, hedge, field and garden are found loaded like Christmas hampers. From the thick serge fetters of winter clothing people walk free as though suddenly pardoned. Out of hiding at last they caress the air, pull it about them like silk, nibble it, drink it, and splash it over their bodies like children discovering water. Children and birds, so long subdued, suddenly populate the outdoor world, fighting, scuffling, flying cries and whistles, stretching their antics to the extremes of daylight. It is the easy, generous, overwhelming time, when life seems to rise like a soufflé. For everyone now there is sap in the blood: grass shoots, wheat swells, plump petals break open, all nature comes to a head. It is a time for short, sharp happy sounds, for long and languorous silences, for idling by water and lying on one's back, for smelling the good in the ground, for forgiveness, love and skimming off the cream, and for examining again in a bee's-eye trance the mesmeric centres of flowers, where still lie preserved the bright drugs of childhood that recall no other world than this.

The Thirties

The teenage bracket, like the licensing laws, is an arbitrary defin-
ition. You don't measure a marrow by clocks or the calendar – when
it's big enough, you eat it.

We of the thirties were late developers, and the reasons, no
doubt, were various. We had already rejected the fripperies of the
twenties, were more austere, more self-denying. Our gramophones
had horns and we wound them by hand. We bicycled against the
wind. Our days were longer than days are now, our pressures less
hysteric. Teenagers today are said to grow bigger earlier, but we,
being poor, were less subject than they are to the artificial fertilizers of big business panders. We were reflective, slow and half in
love with our youth. Consequently I remained a teenager till late in
my twenties. Some of my contemporaries are teenagers still.

This then is a report from a cloudy decade, part-Byronic and
almost wholly forgotten. The time between wars, pre-nuclear and
innocent, which no subsequent teenagers can know. The most
tragic decade of the century, perhaps, because the young then were
full of hope. In spite of the shadows of the oncoming doom we
were confident we could resist it.

We were not to know, till the late 1930s, that we had lived
through the last days of peace. It is only now, of course, that I can
talk so knowingly. I'd no idea what was up at the time. I was a
green country youth when the thirties began, uninstructed and
more than usually naïve. Later I became involved in most of the
myths of the time – but this almost entirely by accident.

In 1931 I was a small-town office boy, earning 7s 6d a week. I
spent my spare time in my snug home village or cycling over

hilltops in search of love. Born twenty years earlier, in that cut-off valley, I might have ended as head clerk or farmer. But the whispers were stirring: faint whispers already were arriving from the outside world. A threepenny cinema thrived in the town. Crystal wireless sets crackled at night. I picked up the music of the Savoy Orpheans; heard Bernard Shaw asking 'Whither Britain?' At the local library I discovered the works of James Joyce, D. H. Lawrence, Huxley and Lenin. I started a dance band, and began to talk posh.

My girlfriends were suitably confused.

As I stretched myself, the village shrank like a corset. It was time to get out and go. So I left home one morning and started walking to London. The journey took me a month. On the long road to London I joined a procession of tramps carrying bundles and billy-cans. At night we brewed tea by the grassy roadsides and they told me about the depression. There were nearly two million unemployed in Britain at that time, and these men were part of that number. They crowded the roads, just aimlessly walking. They were not going anywhere particularly.

I arrived in London in the summer and got a job straight away on a building site. This was largely through the influence of the beautiful daughter of a communist agitator. In return for her favours I was required to join the 'movement' – a debt which I owe her still.

London at that time seemed almost nineteenth century. Dusty, down-at-heel, secure. Wages were low (if you were luckily in work), but life was cheap and easy. A tot of whisky for 6d, a 6d seat in a cinema, cigarettes twenty for 9d – as a builder's labourer earning £2 a week I lived the life of Reilly. At weekends I walked the streets of Soho, bought foreign newspapers which I couldn't read, studied art books at Zwemmer's, smoked Mexican cigars, and played the tables in the amusement arcades. Even the arcades wore an air of innocence then, unlearned as yet in the sweet uses of iniquity. The virginal pin tables, their springs unbent, showered the skilful with cigarette prizes. (No wonder teenagers today, forced to play without hope, take their occasional revenge with a sledgehammer.)

In London those were also the great days of jazz, newly come, like the pin tables, from America; not the pale pocket troubadours of today's TV but the large group-bands of Duke Ellington and Armstrong, whose imitators crowded the music halls.

After a year, the job finished, and I looked about me and felt free to explore the world. There was a taste of peace like cream on the air. The world's frontiers were still wide open. There were rumours from China and Abyssinia, but I for one didn't heed them. I knew one foreign word, the Spanish for 'water'. I decided to go to Spain. I landed in Vigo with £2 in my pocket, a blanket and a violin. For thirteen months I wandered happily through the country, as unaware as an illiterate clown. I'd come, without knowing it, to the great showdown, to the heart of the thirties' tragedy.

The Spanish Civil War found me trapped in a village on the coast near Malaga. Through the dust of the battle came a neat British destroyer to take off its nationals. Tattered tramp though I was, bearing no more than a fiddle, I was piped aboard to a salute by officers. It was probably one of the last occasions when a British passport (signed John Simon) could be afforded such an honour. Very soon the pace was to grow too hot for such elegant niceties.

Back in England I could see what the Spanish Civil War meant. Here was an exercise in repression, and a flesh-and-blood testing ground for the techniques of totalitarian war. Feeling personally involved, I returned to Spain, crossing the Pyrenees in a December blizzard. In the International Brigade I realized at last that I was not alone in this fight. Many others of my age had made the same journey: teenagers from America, Britain, Europe, had come for the last romantic war.

Ill fed and ill armed, many of these young men died, the survivors returned home to ignominy. There were no medals from this war, no listing of the fallen among the names of 'our glorious dead'. But to me this seems to have been the last time that the young had a cause they could believe in and could fight from the heart. In spite of their belief, they were defeated – and in their defeat the thirties perished. The world war followed as night the day, and no teenager has since recovered from it.

As-You-Were-Only-Better

They remember me best as I went away, more than a quarter of a century ago. I left as a turnip-faced grinning oaf, and returned last year, a bag-eyed poet, having in the meantime written a book about them. 'Better mind what you say. He'll put you in writing. Done it before. His poor old mother . . .'

Of course one should never have gone in the first place. It is never really forgiven you. And to revisit one's roots calls from an upside-down posture which too often proves that the plant is broken.

After twenty-five years I find the main changes in me and in the villagers' view of me, but the village itself has come through the revolutions of that time with fewer abrasions than I would have expected.

The place is called Slad and lies some two miles from Stroud in a bent and secretive valley. The valley is steep, and usually running with rain, and some say you can't sleep, in really typical weather, for the noise of snails crawling under low bridges. There used to be cloth mills along the valley bottom, sturdy and prosperous places, but they were all washed away in a great night storm in the early nineteenth century.

I lived in this village until I was twenty and till then knew no other world. I remember it as a place of long steamy silences, punctuated by the sounds of water, by horses' hooves and mowing machines, sleepy pigeons and mooning cows. Of the thirty-odd families living in the straggling cottages, some worked on the farms, some at the mills in Stroud, but most were in service to the Squire. Wages were small, and families large, and there was a tendency to live off the land – wild fruit was bottled, blackberries gathered, pigs kept, fowls raised, rabbits hunted, pigeons trapped, and flowery wines home-brewed in abundance. There was also an intense and vivid communal life, much preferred to outside allurements, with choir-outings, concerts, harvest festivals, feasts, penny-dances and junkets galore. The neighbouring villages were thought to be full of savages and we beat them if they came our way; Stroud was the market, but shark-infested; in any case transport was poor. For the most part we stayed in our tight green valley, as snug as beans in a pod.

How is it now? Visually it's changed very little, maybe a bit better scrubbed round the lintels, but the village still lies in its tree-crammed corner folded deep in the valley's cool. People move about more, most have some kind of car, and will visit the neighbouring villages with impunity. But the long steamy silences can still recur, when everybody seems to have taken cover like moles. There are fewer children, but much better dressed, and fewer, if any, rabbits, and the stretches of common where they once both swarmed are now overgrown with brambles. Living is tidier, more genteel, more opulent; the pet dog has replaced the pig, the wild plum and apple are left to rot on the bough, the fat blackberry gluts the hedgerow ungathered. With the fading Church and the decayed Big House much of the old communal life has gone.

Certain traditional evils have also gone with it – the damp and the cold, poverty, malnutrition, epidemics and early death. Better farming, better shops, better jobs and more money have brought the best changes of all. There is less hunger now, less sheer animal drudgery, people have time to straighten their backs.

Until recently the village lived by oil lamps and wood fires, and cottage windows glowed warm in the dark. Now electricity has come, with its crazy cat's cradle of pylons, and the place is bright as a surgeon's knife. One must approve of this; one can also regret; much has been gained but something lost – the shadows in the corner which fed the poetry of children, and a certain thousand-year-old self-sufficiency (for instance, when lightning cut the current the other morning many cottagers couldn't even make a cup of tea).

Electricity and piped water are common boons now, but the villagers have been busy with other improvements. These are the details of change, invisible from a distance, but part of the modern purge. Broken-down old cottages have been stiffened with concrete, roofs rain-proofed for the first time in centuries. The family car has condemned many an ivy-clad wicket gate (together with the grandmother it used to prop up) in favour of jazzy contraptions – metal tubing smart enough for an aerodrome.

Cottage interiors, too, are getting a vigorous clean-up, as though they were relics of a past best forgotten. Old kitchen ranges, once shrines of the family, are being bricked up like mad relations, heirloom furniture replaced by bird-leg contemporary, velvet curtains by surgical plastic, family photographs and daguerreotypes thrown out and burnt in place of china Bambis and celluloid ducks. Some are even taking the bare Cotswold wall, which perhaps had shamed their kitchen for years, covering it with plaster and hanging it with wallpaper made from coloured photographs of a bare Cotswold wall. This quaint improvement, becoming increasingly popular, is known as the Wall Game or As-You-Were-Only-Better.

Yet in spite of flashier pleasures, and a reasonable restlessness, and the insistent moving-in of the world, the village remains essentially a village, separate as it ever was. A definite though invisible frontier surrounds it and those outside are not quite of God's choosing. The village and its lore are still the world's centre, the beginning and the end of truth, and everything that comes from outside is rung on the local stones before its genuineness can even be considered. Those who thought that the television and wireless might obliterate identities will find the local accent unaffected. Children speak it as well as their elders, and it remains untainted save for formal occasions.

Things I Wish I'd Known at Eighteen

If only I had known that those strange, complicated, romantical, remote, magic and mysterious creatures who dominated my waking and sleeping were quite simple and uncomplex after all. Girls! They sustained me in a state of anguish and of torment when I was an office boy in Stroud, new-washed as wool and wet behind the ears, waiting to walk out and walk away one midsummer morning.

I remember Edna down the road saying: 'But Laurie, I don't know what you're making all the fuss about. Take me down from this pedestal. I'm really quite ordinary.' Touching remark – she was quite right, of course.

And I remember cycling thirty miles to Worcester to sit all night in the rain shriving my soul outside a girl's window with a bag of plums. I was enchanted by her Irish beauty. The bag got wet. The plums fell out. And she married a garage man in the end.

'I dreamt of you one April night . . . when the moon in silv'ry splendour dight . . . hung poised in a realm of clouds. And all around her, her courtiers in a crowd – the stars – were gathered . . .' I wrote this pushing the bike up Painswick Hill. 'And as I dreamt, you came . . . floating across the broad pale flame of the Milky Way . . . to where I lay . . .' Oh it goes on! I think that's enough. I never put it on paper. You wrote in your head then.

But it was a fruitful ignorance in one sense. Her glow, her unattainability, were the source of all my endeavours at the time. And who knows, without such practice I might not have got into Pseuds Corner in *Private Eye*.

There are many other things. I could play the fiddle rather well, but longed to play the piano. I wish I'd learned another language. It would have broadened my reading. Though at that time I did most of my reading at bookshop shelves – several pages a day till I got through the entire stock. You see I only earned 10s a week. Five went to my mother. A shilling for a meat tea on Saturdays – looking for girls of course – and I spent 1s 3d on an ounce of very fine tobacco that had to last the week.

I wish I could have whistled when I was eighteen – whistled properly. I wish I'd learned to swim. I still can't tie my shoelaces – I have to wear slip-on shoes. I wish I'd learned to run downstairs using both legs. I only use the left leg and fetch the right along. It would be nice to be like those young executives coming out of government offices in films – trip-trip-trip down the steps. My co-ordination is still frightful.

Similarly, I can't use the telephone. I didn't actually speak on the phone till I was seventeen. I had to report a fault on the office line. When the girl said, 'Hello – can I help you?' I blushed and hung up speechless. I still find it inhibiting.

Another regret – perhaps it's common – I wish I'd been aware quite what a fool one makes of oneself at that age. You have this blind belief that you've discovered sex, truth, idealism, the sharpness of questioning the world, rebellion. You don't realize that you are repeating the questing and rebellion of every generation and you say, 'God – those old ones seem to have no idea how we feel.'

Well, they have a very good idea. The old have felt it all, and suffered, and been heroes at the barricade, and have got over it. The young don't know that the old are merely them. If they humiliate the old they humiliate themselves. It is necessary to question at eighteen and to put up all those ideals to be shot down again – so long as they don't think they were the first to have them.

Oh, the blankness at that age . . . the prejudices . . . *you know* . . . about the villains of this world. Or the ones you thought were villains. It's marvellous to believe you are the white knight and that those are the black dragons coming over the hill to destroy all that is good. Later you discover that there are no clearly divided goods and evils. The more I've lived the more I've realized that even the best of us are capable of cruelty if we think it's in a good cause. Even the worst have gentleness occasionally. People on the whole are better than you think. There is no black and white – just a pathetic greyness in which everyone is trying to find solutions.

I wish I'd known at eighteen just how my mother felt. I gave her a lot of silence in my teens . . . didn't talk to her enough . . . didn't listen at the time when the others had gone away and I was the only boy in her life. Possibly there were times when she wished to tell me about her state of health or about the cruelties of luck that dogged her. I tried to catch up later on when it was too late for comfort. I wish I'd had the confidence and optimism to know that she would never want.

In those days our world was bounded by those hilltops. Our frontier was three miles away and we seldom crossed it. It's just as well I did walk out. Otherwise I would have been so embraced by this voluptuous countryside that I would have gained no experience of life whatever.

When I even doubted my capacity to make contact with the other sex – unaware that I would become a rather successful, rather tubby man of middle age – if only I could have been reassured by some fairy godmother – or Madame – that with my little pencil I would be able to feed and clothe these two great glowing engines of health.

It would have made life easier if I had been told: 'Relax, boy . . . relax! You're going to make it. You're going to marry one of the most beautiful women in western Europe. You're going to have this lovely daughter.'

Chelsea Towards the End of
the Last War

This is not an anecdote but a memoir of a place and a time – empty Chelsea toward the end of the last war.

I was shaving one morning when the mirror before me suddenly cracked from side to side, at the same time there was a clap of thunder and the sound of some huge roaring vehicle withdrawing in the sky. It was summer, 1944, and the grounds of Chelsea Royal Hospital had that morning been hit by a German rocket. There were no warnings for they had arrived faster than sound and you heard the bomb explosion first and then the bomber going away.

There was something especially macabre and symbolic about the rockets on London that summer; the tension had gone out of the air raids, there was no waiting now, and people arrived before you knew they were coming.

I lodged in a house in a square just off the King's Road – a quiet residence where the landlord and his wife had often gone to bed when I came home from work at nine o'clock in the evening. The girl who rented the room next door overslept regularly and would go to work naked in the morning, just wearing a mackintosh and carrying a basket of clothes so that she could get dressed later on in the train.

Chelsea was seedy, calm and semi-rustic at that time, with the charm of old paint and large undusted houses. Many had been deserted by their owners and were the haunt of cats and lovers, drunken soldiers on leave, and sometimes all three together.

Chromium, Coca-Cola and cannabis had not yet touched King's Road; in many ways it resembled a provincial high street of last century, full of tea shops, greengrocers and family butchers, though the butchers' windows showed only cardboard cut-outs of sheep. There were also shops selling glass jewellery, billy-cans, striped utility suits, and sealed jars of chopped carrots and rhubarb.

There were really not many people about at that time: a number of old activists, war artists and camouflage painters, the widows of artists and vivid ex-models, squeezing out their monthly bottle of gin.

It was the fag end of the war, a quiet conspiratorial time with no secret lives; we were all in it, and by now we knew most things about each other – we shared and stuffed ourselves on them. There was also that all-pervasive sense of eroticism that goes with the boredom of war, that freewheeling fantasizing that goes with displaced persons who are displaced through no fault of their own. The girls and women fell upon the few men with an urgent and hungry disdain. They tidied the rooms of the bachelors and cooked for them. They took our shirts home at weekends and washed them.

For a treat I used to take my girls to the café across the road from The Markham Arms, a long crowded old room of pews and rusty tea cooked in a sort of steam turbine at the end of the room. One ate squares of burnt toast tasting of oil-fired lino, and the scented jam was poured from a bottle. Their bubble and squeak had the bulk and leafy interest of the Gutenberg Bible. Their kippers were the best I've ever known. Was that the last genuine eating house in Chelsea, I wonder, before the whole place began to fall to pizzas? The Pheasantry was another restaurant, but slightly better class, where you could dine for five shillings.

Imagine Chelsea as it was, with no parked cars in the street. The long mellow vista of terrace houses with their pavements running smooth and uncluttered, and the streets wider and clear to the eye as they were designed to be. The quiet of the country seemed to occupy the area at that time. The square gardens ran slowly and disordered through their seasons without the help of municipal workers.

After sundown there were no lights in streets or houses and the primeval darkness came back to London, a darkness which cleared the sky of its raw, neon-flecked glow and returned the sight of stars and the moon to the city. Flower-seeds blew in and thrived on the bombsites and owls sang in the midnight blue. It was a time of strange peace that the war had given.

The Queen's Elm

It is 274 paces from my doorstep, slightly more if the wind blows from the east – a huge blank-faced corner building whose dart-playing public bar is entered from the Fulham Road and its saloon bar from the more classy Old Church Street. Its small swinging sign shows a crowned Queen Elizabeth standing alone in a pasture beside a diseased-looking elm tree.

A natural site for a pub; one has stood here for more than three hundred years, though its association with the Virgin Elizabeth and an elm is arguable. A Chelsea vicar, writing on local history, records that Her Majesty and 'her host', on their way to visit Lord Burleigh of Brompton Hall, took shelter under the elm during a downpour. 'Let this henceforth be called "The Queen's Tree",' Elizabeth is quoted as quothing – which one can't help suspecting, under the circumstances, to be a dubiously pompous remark.

Nevertheless, it is known that a tavern called 'The Queen's Tree' stood on this spot in 1667, dominating the crossroads (one running from the river to Hyde Park, the other from the City to Fulham Village) and refreshing the travellers stopping at the tollgates. This humble hostelry probably disappeared with the rubbing out of the tollgates. The present Queen's Elm, in all its non-committal grandeur, was built in 1914, just in time for our present licensing scramble.

'The Elms', as it is so often fondly but incorrectly referred to in poems, novels, confessions, dry exile, deathbed reminiscences or moments of what-shall-we-do? ennui, has been my London local for over twenty years. First, because it was the nearest pub in any direction from where I lived; and later, in 1958, when Sean Treacy put his grip on it, because it became the kind of place I should even go several more paces out of my way to reach.

The inexplicable, often inexcusable, but inimitable Treacy served his apprenticeship at nearby Finch's, and when he took over The Elms he was still the thin pale western Irishman we had known up the road, with his flair for collecting dedicated drinkers around him, the distinguished, the notorious, the nameless. With his move from the other place he trailed a number of these customers with him, who at first dithered between their two difficult loyalties, but later became the hard core of Sean's new establishment. And the thin white lad prospered. And The Elms filled up. And over the years Sean plumped out his feathers, purpled, toughened, mixed his drink and friends with astonishing results, and developed that instantly recognizable though slightly bellicose magnetism which now makes him like no other landlord in London. He is a ruthless professional, but drinks on the customers' side of the bar, scrupulously standing his round. He also has another priceless quality of his trade. He never forgets a face, a name, an anecdote, or a bounced cheque.

It is difficult to define the exact nature of Sean Treacy's effect on the extraordinary popularity of The Elms. He can often be absent-mindedly moody, egocentric, intolerant, full of oaths, a man of bulk and noise and sudden shouts of laughter (usually following his own jokes). He is also a unique, warm-blooded and generous host; he draws people together and refurbishes their self-esteem, and most regulars will admit that when Sean is absent from the bar, a fire – metaphorically and literally – is out.

The Elms itself, to put it mildly, is not noticeable for its distinction. There are any number of smarter, flashier, more comfortable, more elegant pubs around. Enter the saloon bar door and you are more than likely to knock over a wooden coat-stand covered with broken hooks. The floor is bare except for a rippled lino of an indefinable age and colour. The long curved counter is topped with a similarly mysterious, though somewhat brighter, substance. The place has a marked absence of cosiness and style. The only concession to chic is the collection of original Jak cartoons on the tomato-red walls and Sean's valuable frieze of antique pipes. But what we all know – and this may be one of the explanations of its attractions – is that the Elms is simply a spacious and relaxed drinking area where the lions and Christians of the world, the hawks and the doves, take it for granted they can mix in temporary and bloodless armistice, as they might as passengers on the Ark.

Something unpredictable has grown up over the years, the certainty and variety of what one will find there, under the unwritten guarantee of Sean's presence. 'It's not the comfort, it's not the service, it's certainly not the prices,' a regular will tell you. 'I just reckon it's the people you get.'

'You know you'll always meet someone you know, even if he's only the biggest cad south of Tring.'

The Elms is an arena, a general meeting place; or to put it another way, it has become the chosen drinking hole for several hundred divers types who know they can come here pacifically when the thirst is on them and enjoy its traditional, almost atavistic, protection before returning to the jungle to take up again their separate roles as predators or panic victims.

For Sean Treacy's customers must be the most varied and constantly evolving bunch ever to gather together under one tavern roof. They include diplomats, doctors, drifters, dukes, professional golfers, Fleet Street gossips, goons, cops and robbers, judges (two), painters and decorators, chair-menders, clerks, actors, poets, film directors, freaks, flamboyant princes of King's Road boutiques, Russians, Basques, Nigerians, Zulus, musclemen, models, exquisite lesbians, spies, cancer research professors, professors of painting and sculpture, fashion photographers, chaps who'll mend your car, your roof or your mind, and a sprinkling of local priests whose brief appearances are bright and jolly as Pentecostal flames.

Behind the bar the paid help, busy among their levers and optics, can be as diverse as the customers, having numbered among them over the past few years retired Olympic swimmers, diminutive Corsican crooks, out-of-work pop singers, peeresses, bachelors of science and the law, whiskered Turkish sponge-divers, bare-bellied maidens and that mutton-chopped doyen of all barmen, 'Laurie'.

I suppose what is typical of most pubs, and is certainly true of The Elms, is that no night's atmosphere is ever the same. The long cast of characters, with a few immovable exceptions, is not always present, thank God. The blend may, and does, vary, but strangely the essential feel remains familiar; blindfold, you would always know you were there.

Go in early. The place is almost empty, the fire unlit, the three or four solitaires reading their newspapers. 'No one here tonight,' says the barman, looking up at the clock and sniffing. After the second half-pint you may think of moving elsewhere, even of going home. But this almost always is made impossible. The door pushes open and the first of the night's outriders appear, shakingly sober, quiet-spoken, white-faced. A great deal depends, at this moment, on whether Sean arrives too and is able to stir up the others with a few aggressive provocations. If he is late, the night's required celebration of gregarious amnesia may sometimes be sparked off by someone else, say by the loud hazy shout of a Fleet Street cartoonist who has been hard at it all day in the clubs, or by the emblazoned entrance of a temporarily idle actor, well known, well heeled and well lit. Then there is a slapping of backs, a sharp rise in temperature, and a glittering scatter of fairy gold.

Now in the great doglegged space of the saloon bar the night's mazed pattern begins to emerge. Jeans, jewels, T-shirts, furs, Austin Reed suits, and donkey jackets, the customers wander, gather, clot in groups, dilate, contract, spill over. A girl slips her hand from one to another's. A retired warrior orders a triple brandy. The street door opens again admitting warm waves of erotic air as more girls arrive with their bushy men. Couples meet, melt, accuse, forgive, endlessly exchange permutations.

Suddenly the sad empty lino, the flickering fire, the bored barmen are overwhelmed. The Elms is filling, is full, elbow-to-elbow, wall-to-wall, topped by a sea of open glistening mouths. The famous, the lonely, the suicidal, even the bores are now joined in a marriage of careless minds. This is the time for extravagance, wit, generosity, intrigue, time for vast vegetable loves to grow. With returned exiles from Malta groping for the names and knees of old girlfriends. Amateur Mafia stroking each other's fifty-quid shirts. The solemn spoof players joined in their ritual circle; and the friendly psychopath in the corner, watching. And always, in spite of the noise, of arguments of novelists from the Bronx, dancers from Melbourne, scuba-divers from Tripoli, you will observe, occupying some of the few red seats by the windows, and gazing at each other in silence over their minced beef and lager, an assortment of beautiful creatures one has never seen before, who have blown in like drifting summer seeds, and will drift out again soon and never be seen again, but will be almost exactly replaced tomorrow.

One may have meant to leave early; but the door is a revolving trap. One is caught by a stream of continuous entrances, by friends airborne from earlier parties. 'You're not going. Nonsense. This is Elsa from Oslo. Come over here. You're putting on weight. They tell me you still cheat at billiards. Reggie Bosanquet's livid.' One is drawn back into a warm and whisky-fumed womb.

As it grows late, Sean Treacy will have gathered round him now all the chance potpourri of the evening – perhaps a composer, a footballer, a policeman off-duty, a couple of actors, a hall porter from Kensington. Head down, bullish, his drinks lined up before him, his conversation ballooning with oaths and laughter, he is pulling his friends together with a series of sidesteps and retreats, knowing that it is up to him to bring the curtain down. 'Should have gone home hours ago. Jan will bloody well kill me. Have one for the road – my turn – the last.'

The lights flicker, go off, come on again. The crowded bar begins to sort itself out. Sean tells one more story. About Lester Piggott and the Pope. We've heard it before; no matter. We have reached that peak of desperate relish for each other. There is no movement towards the door. A theatre critic suddenly begins to blunder about like a blind and livid beetle. He is followed by a retired general with that measured poise of one who knows his eyes are crossed and his legs are going.

The final lights go down, accompanied by a sort of sigh of withdrawal, an exhalation of energy, appreciation and regret. Something artificial yet unique is about to be switched off, our intravenous feedback to adolescent euphoria and power. What we've known tonight at The Elms we have not known elsewhere, could not have known elsewhere, and may never quite know again.

To the uninitiated, all public houses are alike, but few are without shades of difference. Indeed, many are the specialized haunts of like-feathered birds – journalists, actors, sailors, city clerks, the blue-jeaned and beaded brethren. The Queen's Elm is probably unlike any other in that it scoops in all types at once. It is also a rallying place and a rendezvous, a point of departure and return. Known faces will disappear from years – to Zanzibar, Belize, on cryptic trips to the Oman or the Atlas – and when they come back they'll consider their return scarcely official until they have first made a call at The Elms. A girl will make a good marriage, be swept away to the shires, then suddenly turn up without warning, quietly and plumply divorced, ready to start out her life again. In the stormy seas of many, The Elms floats like a carrier, to some a refuge, to others a launching pad.

The pub, more recently, has developed a valuable sideline in providing a kind of market for its many writers and painters. This shoot of the business may have sprouted casually and unnoticed in the poor old days, some fifteen years ago, when the late Paddy Kavanagh and I, in an upstairs room, used to swap our poems for tots of whisky. Later I exploited this ground by going round the bars at Christmas and flogging my books from a carrier bag. In this way we discovered a curious but obvious truth, that people who would never dream of going into a bookshop were quite happy to buy several volumes over a drink. A bookshop may properly complain that it is not licensed to sell beer – but there are also a number of other things not in its power to provide: geniality, coal fires, often the company of the author, and the opportunity of buying your Christmas presents, over a slow pint of Guinness, late on a Saturday night.

This side of The Elms' booze-and-book-industry was formally consolidated by Sean Treacy himself when, a couple of years ago, he too broke into print with the publication of his memoirs: *A Smell of Broken Glass*. He keeps a large stock of this work in the wine cellars from which he regularly replenishes the saloon bar shelves, standing them in rows among bright bottles of Jameson and Jack Daniels together with the latest works of other Elms regulars – Marshall Pugh, Maureen Duffy, Digby Durrant, Peter Smiley, paperbacks by Jak, and by myself.

Moreover, the room upstairs, neglected for years, is again being put to good use; people come and go talking of Michelangelo, of Liz Frink, Gerald Scarfe, Robert Buhler, Bill Thomson, Trevor Willoughby, Norman Stevens and others, selections of whose work are regularly on show there, regularly on sale, or both.

The Elms wastes nothing, for upstairs there will also be, from time to time, meetings for the preservation of real beer, for author's lending rights, for the exchanging of medals by foreign govern-ments in exile, meetings for visiting stock-breeders, and of course book-launching parties – one of which should celebrate any day now the publication of Sean Treacy's scurrilous new novel, *Shay Scally and Manny Wagstaff*.

Sean Treacy is not bog-Irish, stage-Irish or even saloon-bar-Irish; he is too complex and unclassifiable for any such labels. He was born in Galway, of stern but intelligent parents, and was brought up in the small crossroads village of Glenamaddy. In his youth he took part in shebeens, wakes, duck-shooting, fist-fighting and other such west Irish pleasures of forty years ago, and was later reluc-tantly educated at St Jarlath's College.

For five years he was a pilot in the Irish Army Air Corps, where he earned a reputation for unpredictability, dandyism and bilin-gual raciness in English and Gaelic. Finally he broke free and grounded himself to start a career in pubs, beginning as a learner-barman in a tough Cockney-Irish house in Shepherd's Bush, where the lean blond good-looking young man so quickly caught on to the nuances of pub-keeping (a blend of conviviality, sharp-eyed realism and the ability to quell riots without shedding of blood) that within a year he was managing the famous Fulham Road Finch's.

The Queen's Elm is the only pub in London which, to my mind, serves as a true, thoroughly comprehensive Rialto. Where else, in one evening, could you be greeted by your Irish landlord with a Gaelic insult and a double scotch, consult a doctor, tussle with your bank-manager, drink with a TV comic, arrange a poetry reading and tickle a nurse, then be invited to supper by a Jermyn Street nightclub owner and finally leave the bar with more money in your pocket than you went in with, to the ringing farewells of the pub-manager, Sliwo, a Babylonian Christian from Baghdad?

The Magic of Water

I discovered water at the age of four, at the mouth of our cottage pump. I remember it not as a thing merely for washing and scrubbing, but as a plaything with a brilliant life of its own. One could pump it in pure blue gulps out of the ground, and it came out sparkling like liquid sky. It broke or ran, or quivered in a jug, or weighted one's clothes with cold. I found you could drink it, draw with it, swim beetles across it, or fly it in bubbles in the air. You could bury your head in it, and open your eyes, and see the old bucket buckle, and hear your caught breath roar, and smell the sharp lime from the ground. It was a plaything of magic, which you could confine or scatter, but never burn or destroy.

Perhaps none of us lose that early passion for water, for we are bound to it by ancestral cords. The sight and sound of it cures our minds, and most of our pleasure seems to be ordered around it. When we wallow in our baths, is it just to get clean, I wonder, or is the pleasure something deeper than that, an indulgent return to the weightless peace of the womb, or to the warm shallow lapping of those primeval seas where all life is said to have begun?

Water has a thousand pleasures and a thousand faces, and it is the most versatile of all the elements. Fire is masculine, monotonous, blundering, crude; water is feminine and far more subtle. It can offer the heaped-up power of a murdering ocean, or the miniature frolic of a municipal fountain, the pitiless sledgehammer of an annihilating flood, or the bucolic vacancy of a summer duck pond. Water is the puddle just big enough for a small boy's boot, the thundering curtains of Niagara Falls, the star in a snowflake, the mist on a cobweb, the protective arm round an ancient city. It is the sting on the lips from a hill-cold spring, the chisel that cut out the shape of Britain, the singing spout of a kettle, the last cry of the man in the desert.

Water is all things to all men, and most of them good. Most of all, it is a great healer and pacifier. We do not go to the river to fight or make trouble, but to sit and gaze at it, or splash about. Man makes a special noise when he gets near water – you hear it at the seaside and in the bathroom – a kind of wordless, ageless, happy yell, the cry of a child in the arms of his mother.

Water is the great innocence left on earth, something which no one so far has spoiled. Our littered lands may stretch right to the coast, but no one has yet put a scar on the sea.

The Lake District

It resembles from the air a kind of rough-cut jewel hanging from the narrow throat of Scotland, a jagged cameo of crumpled green with blue slivers of lake. It is a unique and ancient part of Britain and was forged by fire and ice. Its primeval slates, washed from lost Atlantis, were split open by giant volcanoes, convulsed by earthquakes, scarred by glaciers, folded in fells and valleys in whose landlocked pockets gathered the lakes and tarns still fed by the Atlantic rains.

The result is a landscape of miniature perfection, a thirty-mile circle of silence, a small, closed world neither Scottish not English but quite separate from the country around it. By its nature it remains a fortress region and has developed distinct and alone. Ancient Britons lived here, Roman troops passed by, even the Welsh once tried to colonize it. But the people who made this district their own were the Vikings from Scandinavia. In the mountains, forests and long, still lakes, they saw reflections of their northern homes. So they settled here and wrote their language across the landscape. Study the signposts, with their becks, fells and dales, and you are reading a Norseman's lexicon. The dalesmen themselves, with their craggy faces, their dialect gritty as rock, are for the most part living descendants of Vikings.

But the Lake District is something more than names; it is a place of subtle details, of shifting light and boiling rain clouds, of skies seen in endless mirrors. Of old granite bridges humpbacked like sheep, of stone-walled rocky lanes, of whitewashed cottages, ruined mills and gaunt farms full of hot-eyed dogs. It is a region of mystery and ancient marks, giants' caves and holy wells, of standing stones raised to forgotten spirits, of British forts and Roman roads. Here was once a rough and simple living, with farming, pig-keeping and sheep, with mining, quarrying, weaving and spinning, split by occasional outbreaks of violence. Signs of that human life remain but are overshadowed by those other presences – the round-backed fells, silent as gods, bearing the sky on their many horizons, and radiating from them the lakes, like petals changing colour every hour of the day.

Until 1800, this was unvisited country, save for the occasional Scottish raiders. Then the poet Wordsworth, himself a native, gave the spirit of the Lakes to the world. What he and his fellow poets saw remains to be seen today – the march of light across lake and mountain that gave man a grandiose new vision of nature.

The Lakeland is like a spectacular sunset – you must simply see it for yourself. Most of the fells can only be reached on foot, but the reward of this travail is a cloud-pressed pride, a memorable sense of achievement and such great gulps of air and distance and serenity that you will never be the same again.

To visit the Lake District with some system, it is best to make plans beforehand. Enter by Kendal, on the Carlisle railroad, and from there go to Lake Windermere. A passenger steamer will carry you to Ambleside in the very heart of the region. With a pair of stout shoes, a good staff and a compass you can climb to the top of Old Man. Then later to Ullswater, over the Kirkstone Pass, with the mass of Helvellyn around you – from the peak of which you can see into Scotland and out to the Irish Sea. Next, to Wordsworth's Grasmere, then north to Keswick (commanding Skiddaw) and Derwentwater. Finally south through Borrowdale, over Honister Pass, brushing Great Gable and Scafell Pike, to make your own way down to the pine-woody shores of Buttermere and Crummock Water.

The district is not exclusive to mountain climbers; there are good motor roads for those without legs. There is also bicycling, camping, sailing and fishing – even cockfighting (though this is illegal).

Spring is the best time, with the hills slate green and Wordsworth's daffodils fringing the lakesides. In the fall the bracken is copper red; in winter the wild geese come. But should you go in summer, make it the third Thursday in August and you can follow the Grasmere Sports – with Cumberland wrestling, the trailing of hounds and the famous Fell Race to the top of Butter Crags and back, one of the most exhausting tests in the world.

Man has spoiled much in the last hundred years, but the mountains and the sea still resist him. So does the Lake District. It is not very big. But it still reminds us of much we have lost.

Lords of Berkeley Castle

The colours of the walls of the castle – as Vita Sackville-West points out – have been compared to those of dried rose petals mixed with the grey of lavender. When seen through the mellow mists of a late-afternoon summer afternoon, this may strike one as a fair description. In fact, it is deceptively cosy; there is nothing soft about the castle, it is hard, granite-hard, standing out with something of the metallic rustiness of some old engine of war, a punitive system of ramparts which the Berkeley family have maintained through the centuries in order to resist and endure, and at times to command, the onslaught of violent times.

Inside, the fierceness of the castle is a little mitigated; the walls are hung with Brussels tapestries, seascapes and Gainsborough portraits; generations of Berkeley wives have contributed a female and civilizing influence, the floors are covered with fine rugs, and there are tapestry seats and stools woven by a wife of the seventeenth century. The impedimenta of past domesticity survive intact: in the great kitchens, spits and churns and huge lead sinks. But even so, the castle inside is still a little untamed. It is not the graceful interior of a country house, but a series of great rooms connected by narrow staircases and passageways, with doorways which could be held against attack by a few men armed with swords and pikes. Not all the fine mirrors, rich rugs and silver services of succeeding generations can tame the place: as Vita Sackville-West wrote, it is a fortress, an alarming place that exacts a high level of living from the soul.

The raised mount, or rocky outcrop, upon which this Norman castle is built, must have been the site of far older strongholds.

Strategically, it dominated part of the left bank of the tidal Severn, and also connected with ancient sea routes to Ireland, Gaul, Spain and the Mediterranean.

Even earlier in time, when the Severn was young and wide, and ran in a great shining curve from central Wales to the sea, the Vale of Berkeley, through which it passed, was then just a flat marshy jungle overlooked by the Neolithic tribes who lived among the high Cotswold ridges.

The Romans, when they came, found firmer ground in the Vale and set up a station to guard the river crossing. (There are still earthworks near Berkeley called 'Welshman's Castle' – probably a Romano-British defence against Irish pirates.) After the Romans, the Saxons – arriving by land and water, first to pillage and then to settle. It was the great tribe of the Hwicce who overran most of what is now Gloucestershire, and who later, seduced by the fertility of the place, turned their spears and shields into ploughs and crosses and became Christianized farmers and priests.

'Berkeley' was originally an abbey, and the first known reference to it goes back to A D 759, when the presiding Abbot witnessed a deed. 'Beorc lea' is Saxon for 'birch clearing' or 'birchwood'; and in 804 a document mentions the 'Beorclingas'; the 'Men of Berkeley' – or Abbey monks.

This was the dawn of ecclesiastical power, and Berkeley Abbey, at that time, was one of the most substantial landowners in the west. Even in those days Berkeley was a coveted prize, especially among the spiritual heads of the Saxon Church, and when Æthelmund, chief of the Hwicce, was killed in 802, and his widow Ceolburh appointed Abbess of Berkeley, the Abbots of Worcester fumed for nearly a hundred years and were only quietened by the intervention of King Alfred.

Then in 910, the Danes came up the river, destroyed the Abbey and put their own priests into Worcester. Not till now, out of the miasmas of the Severnside mists, do the outlines of Berkeley Castle first begin to emerge.

England at this time was a patchwork of rivalries and relationships – ethnic and political. Saxon chieftains were trying to buy off the Danish raiders, who took the money and also large parts of the country. There were claims to kingship, and counter-claims, guerrilla warfare, treaties, takeovers – while among it all French-speaking Norsemen from Normandy were infiltrating into positions of power and authority.

The Berkeley family stem back into this whirlpool of opportunism, to this critical floodtide in the history of Britain. Their line may be said to have begun with Edward the Confessor, the mild, peaceable mystic, who had kinsfolk among the Normans, and who seemed already resigned to their eventual invasion.

Edward the Confessor's 'staller', or 'horse-thane', was a Saxon noble called Eadnoth, who could be called the true sire of the Berkeley clan. Eadnoth was remarkable in being perhaps one of the few Saxon chiefs to survive the coming of the Norman conquerors. After the Battle of Hastings, he switched his allegiance to William and was allowed a position of military authority. In 1068, he fell fighting against the rebel sons of King Harold, whose grandson, Robert Fitzhardinge, was to be the key figure in the fate of the Berkeleys.

But the first Lord of the West, after the Normans came, was William FitzOsbern, the Earl of Hereford and the Conqueror's defender against the Welsh. FitzOsbern recognized the importance of Berkeley and fortified the place in the eleventh-century Norman manner – not with a castle of stone, but simply a high mound encircled by a moat and crowned with a wooden stockade.

When FitzOsbern returned to France in 1070, he set aside 'five hides' for strengthening the castle, and put in charge his local representative, Roger de Dursley. Roger's family held the 'Castle' during the early struggles for power between the various Norman claimants for the late Conqueror's throne. But they backed Matilda and Stephen, the weaker side, and so in the end lost their vast possessions. Stephen's successful rival, Henry Plantagenet of Anjou, had based himself for a time in Bristol, where his cause received the generous backing of the rich city merchant and reeve, Robert Fitzhardinge, descendant of Eadnoth the Horsethane.

When Henry won his throne, he rewarded his loyal supporter with huge estates down the western edge of the Cotswolds and also with a charter to the Manor of Berkeley. Robert received his prize in 1153 – and his family have held the castle till the present day.

This unique fact of survival might be traced to certain hereditary traits which the first Robert Fitzhardinge showed from the beginning – tact, a sense of compromise, flexibility of mind and wit, and also the talent, when necessary, to lie low and appear invisible when greedy monarchs were out looking for loot.

At least one of these qualities was called upon right from the start; for when Robert Fitzhardinge moved in, he found ex-King Stephen's Roger de Dursley (who had changed his name to Berkeley) still in possession of the castle. Roger was of course thrown out, but he and Fitzhardinge were left with all the elements of a bitter blood feud and rivalry. The dangerous situation was characteristically solved by the arrangement of a double marriage between the houses. Robert Fitzhardinge, in turn, now changed his name to Berkeley, and married his heir, Maurice, to Roger's daughter, Alicia. Then the dispossessed Roger, with what grace he could muster, gave a daughter to another of Robert's sons.

This is how the grandson of the Saxon horsethane found his power as a Norman baron confirmed; as 'Robert de Berkeley' he strengthened the walls of his castle, enjoyed his great possessions in peace, founded St Augustine's Abbey in Bristol, and in due course died and was buried there.

Now began one of the most prolonged, unusual, quixotic, razor-edged yet successful survivals of any of the great houses of Britain. Over eight centuries the castle has been altered, enlarged, been humbled, impoverished or enriched. Sometimes it was a royal plaything, a toy, a tease, to be snatched away from the owners and held in a mood of mischief or spite, or tossed as a bauble to some temporary court favourite. Sometimes it was a forgotten pile standing in an unfashionable marsh, a pawn in a battle, or the key to a whole campaign. But throughout the many onsets of danger to this great craggy edifice, standing rose-tinted above the Severn, resolute generations of Berkeleys have successfully clung to its ancient stones, have hovered, circled, stooped and struck, like kestrels defending a threatened nest.

In Robert of Berkeley's long line of heirs and collaterals, one finds almost every type of our landed gentry – from the dull unremembered, the studious and devout, the plain country farmer and fiery squire, to the schemer, eccentric, cultured patron of the arts, military hero, rakehell and bounder. Many were fortunate enough to live lives of sylvan quiet. Others found their castle placed in the cannon's mouth. But desperate as they were – and must have been – there remains concealed behind all their differences one consistent tenacity of action.

Something of this quality is described by the Berkeleys' historian, Smythe, when writing of Thomas of Berkeley (*c.* 1170–1243): 'Hee soe evenly observed a prudent inclyninge after the strongest powers, that he ever avoyded those Court and Country stormes which in his tyme blewe down many stronger Cedars than himself.' This same Thomas also displayed early the family's knack at consolidating their estates by arranging enclosures, exchanges of ground, and by paring 'the skirts of his chace of Michaell of it Wood by granting in fee many Acres thereof to divers men at three pence, fower pence and six pence the Acre.'

These were tremulous times of political pitch and toss when life and lands so often depended on chance. Thomas's predecessor, for instance, Robert, was nearly destroyed by joining an abortive plot against King John. Then Thomas's successor, Maurice, most elegantly recouped by marrying the daughter of one of King John's bastards, and, in the face of general protest, enclosing more land to the commoners' 'small comfort and still less gaines'.

It was about now that the sulphurous clouds of history began to settle most darkly upon the castle. The story begins at the time of Thomas, first Baron Berkeley, a straightforward loyalist, 'twenty-eight tymes in armes' for his king. He was captured at Bannockburn, freed by ransom, and returned to Gloucestershire to die in peace. But his successor, Maurice, second Baron Berkeley, possibly sniffing winds of advantage elsewhere, gave his monarch no such support.

Edward II, after all, was already in deep trouble with his subjects, having lost Scotland to the Bruce, the respect of his barons, and the allegiance of his queen, Isabelle. Yet he continued to shower estates upon unpopular favourites – particularly Hugh le Despenser. Maurice of Berkeley joined a revolt against the King, was betrayed, and died in chains at Wallingford.

And this is where his son, Thomas, third Baron Berkeley, emerges as one of the most enigmatic and possibly the most treacherous of all the Lords of Berkeley. First, to avenge his father, Thomas became a more devious rebel and married the daughter of Roger Mortimer, the Queen's lover and Edward's usurper. Then, with Mortimer and Queen Isabelle established in power, he recovered all his dead father's lands. By now, King Edward II was on the run in Wales, a disgraced fugitive, with few friends in the land.

He was hounded, captured and, by order of Queen Isabelle, carried to Berkeley Castle. Thomas is said to have received him with every courtesy and kindness. Subsequent events throw some doubt upon this.

In the old keep at the castle there was, and still is, a deep well or dungeon, with stagnant water at the bottom. According to a copy of *The Gentleman's Magazine*, a tame seal was once kept there which slowly devoured all miscreants thrown down to it. A stronger tradition has it that the carcasses of animals (and humans) were regularly dumped in the well, and when any commoner or thief incurred the Lord of Berkeley's displeasure, he was thrown after them, closed in and forgotten. Prisoners of nobler birth, however, received less summary treatment. They were merely placed in a tiny windowless cell which stood above the dungeon and abandoned to the stench of the rotting corpses below.

When the doomed King Edward was brought to Berkeley it was the Queen's intention that he should not leave the castle alive. Early in April 1327 he was shut up in this noisome cell, but five months later, because of his robust constitution, he still had not sickened and died, as was hoped.

At this, Queen Isabelle sent fresh instruction to the castle, demanding some swift conclusion. The King's official jailors at

Berkeley were two imaginative brutes, Sir John Maltravers and Sir Thomas Gurney. On receiving the Queen's message, they acted forthwith; but no one will ever know whether the castle's lord acted with them. The rest is recorded, however: on the night of September 21, the jailors burst into the King's cell, seized him, and pinioned him between two mattresses, then 'a kind of horn or funnel was thrust into his fundament through which a red-hot spit was run up his bowels'. The shrieks of the tortured King were said to have been heard far outside the castle walls; and there are those who say they can be heard today.

Edward II, among other things, was a homosexual, and the manner of his death may have been supposed by his murderers to be one that would appeal to the people's sense of justice and humour. In fact, they were mistaken; the news of the atrocity was received everywhere with horror, and the unpopular Edward rapidly became a martyr.

In fear of the Queen's temper, the Abbots of Bristol and Malmesbury refused to accept the King's body for burial. But John Thokey, Abbot of Gloucester, in a moment of inspired courage or opportunism, immediately sent off to the castle an escort of funereal monks. They found the royal corpse lying abandoned in his cell, naked under a pile of sacking. With sombre pomp they prepared a wagon and horses and proceeded to bring the dead King back to Gloucester. His passage up the Vale was extraordinary. Peasants massed along the route in tears; and when the procession halted at dusk, a few miles from the city, at Standish, a nightlong vigil was held with torches.

Edward was buried near the high altar at St Peter's Abbey, Gloucester, where he rapidly became the centre of a quasi-religious cult. Pilgrims thronged to his tomb from all over the country, and St Peter's modest little Abbey prospered. Soon the monks were able to enlarge it into a major cathedral, while the Abbeys at Malmesbury and Bristol declined. Indeed, it may be true to suppose that much of the splendour of Gloucester Cathedral today may be traced back to that Berkeley murder some 650 years ago. And the carved likeness on the King's sepulchre still bears the look of twisted anguish said to have been copied directly from a contemporary death mask.

Understandably enough, when Edward III succeeded his father, Thomas of Berkeley faced some awkward questions. He kept a cool head, however, and when summoned for trial before Parliament, came up with some prompt though improbable answers. One of these was that he had been ordered out of the castle owing to his 'consistent courtesies' to the King; another that he wasn't there on the night of the murder anyway but lying ill at Bradley, some five miles distant.

Parliament and Edward III accepted his word and acquitted him; he was restored to grace from the edge of doom, fought a few token battles behind his new king's banner, and continued to prosper and extend his lands. But the family historian, Smythe, in spite of his affection for the Berkeleys, felt bound to record one ice-cold fact – that from a careful examination of the household accounts, it was clear that Thomas was at the castle at the time of the murder.

Now the castle was to witness a new twist in British history by seeing the end of the Plantagenets – when a Berkeley marriage into the family of Lord de Lisle, a Lancastrian, brought Henry of Lancaster face to face with Edmund of York.

Thus began that period of national gangsterism cosily named 'The Wars of the Roses', during which the Berkeleys and their castle passed some perilous years. It was a time of reckless opportunism, of king-making-and-breaking, the quick stab in the back, the law of the man in possession.

The Berkeleys' ploy of non-involvement, together with their art of survival, were found suddenly to offer them no protection. The powerful de Lisles, aided by another marriage with the House of Warwick, now had a strong claim to the Berkeley inheritance. But though the de Lisle heirs and their allies held most of the cards, the Berkeleys still had their native wit. Compromise, bribery, more intermarriage was tried, but the de Lisles continued to press down hard. There were years of bitter rivalry between heirs male and heirs general; feuding, raiding and litigation – during which one Lord of Berkeley, on receiving a subpoena, made the messenger eat the parchment, wax seal and all.

The matter was finally settled in a dramatic manner. After a recent plot to seize the castle had frustratingly miscarried, the twenty-year-old Viscount de Lisle, having just inherited the title and its claims, impetuously wrote off a letter to Berkeley's then lord, William, challenging him to decide the affair by a 'meeting of armes'.

Berkeley agreed immediately. Young de Lisle gathered an army of several hundred retainers and pitched his camp on some high ground near Dursley; while foxy Lord William, taking advantage of his position on the Severn crossing, secretly ferried over one thousand bowmen from the Forest of Dean. He hid most of his men, by night, around the approaches to Dursley, and then encamped openly, with a modest following. The next day he called out the local children and told them to climb the treetops if they wanted to see a battle. De Lisle was lured into attacking the Berkeley forces where he ran into ambush at Nibley Green. His army was routed almost immediately, and broke and fled before the watching children; the young Lord himself was shot by Will Black, the Forest Archer, and finished off with a dagger stroke. The Battle of Nibley Green is considered to have been the last private battle in England, and everyone seemed to accept the outcome. Lord de Lisle's young widow was given a pension of £100 a year, and the Lord of Berkeley confirmed in all his disputed possessions.

Following that critical challenge to the continuity of the Berkeleys, William reverted to their tactics of lying low. England was still embroiled in the Wars of the Roses. After the murder of the Princes in the Tower and the accession of Richard III, William sweetened the new monarch with a bribe of thirty-five manors; indeed, he went further and hedged his bets by bribing the Yorkists and Lancastrians simultaneously – 'ayding the one wth men, the other with money, neither of both with his person'. This wily neutrality ensured for William a certain peace, but he was robbed and blackmailed by each of the warring factions every time one or the other of them got the upper hand.

William, twelfth Lord of Berkeley, from having been the victor of Nibley Green, ended by becoming the 'Waste-all' of his huge estates. He had no children, so he entailed to Henry VII all the family's possessions in return for certain privileges and protections. So from his death in 1492, till the death of Henry's eventual successor, Edward VI, in 1553, the Berkeley heirs were dispossessed of their castle and lands and forced to wander in exile about the country.

Smythe paints a touching picture of William's surviving brother, Sir Maurice, who fought to the end of his life – by seeking out flaws in deeds of entailments and conveyances – to repair some of the havoc the 'Waste-all' had caused. 'With a milk white head,' wrote Smythe, 'in his irksome old age of 70. years, in Winter Terms and frosty seasons, with a buckerom bagg stuffed with lawe cases, in early mornings and late evenings walking with his eldest son between the fower Inns of Court and Westmte^r Hall, following his law suites in his own old person . . .'

Berkeley prospered again with the succession of Maurice's son, who inherited forty manors won back by his father's litigations. Henry VIII also created him Baron of Berkeley, by writ, and then capriciously appointed him Lieutenant of Calais – probably just to get rid of him while Henry enjoyed Berkeley's magnificent hunting. The 'Lieutenant' died suddenly in Calais, and was succeeded by his brother, Sir Thomas, who had been knighted on Flodden Field and then forgotten, and had been spending his life as a threadbare Cotswold shepherd, 'without the expectation of inheritance'.

These were the quiet years of rebuilding the estates, when the Berkeleys kept themselves out of sight again. Perhaps one of the last, and most notable, involvements of the castle with history came during the Civil War. Part of the life of Berkeley's long-lived George, nicknamed 'The Harmless', coincided with this uneasy time; and when there appeared to be any danger of his having to take sides, he developed a quick interest in foreign travel. He was caught at home, however, during a critical campaign in the west, when Cromwell's forces suddenly laid siege to the castle. They had already knocked a great hole in one of the walls, when George came to a rapid understanding with the enemy. No heroics – just his promise that if they did no more damage he would swear on oath not to repair the hole. The Parliamentary forces peacefully occupied the castle, and then left quietly after the fall of Bristol. Over three hundred years later the hole is still in the wall – a visible token of the Berkeley's word.

George the 'Harmless', the 'Affable', the 'Peaceful', also loved life, ease and culture. He was a patron of Robert Burton, who dedicated to him (rather incongruously) *The Anatomy of Melancholy*. George's son, also George, helped in the restoration of King Charles II, and was created Viscount Dursley and Earl of Berkeley. Though Royalists, and living in a whirlpool of violent events in which many great names of England went under, the two Berkeley Georges seem to have emerged with characteristically little damage – indeed, with a certain increase in honours and material profit.

Since the Restoration, the castle may be said to have played no profound part in the country's history – except for the fact of its indestructible presence on the banks of the Severn.

But going back over 850 years to Robert Fitzhardinge, much can be picked out from the lives of the succeeding Lords of Berkeley in terms of dash, cunning, endurance, courage, sense of camouflage, and occasional scandal. From the very first, the family were vulnerable to the whims of kings, but they survived every kind of treachery. In medieval days, when a knight held his castle and land by mortgaging his life to his lord, the Berkeleys, though dispossessed at various times almost to the status of herdsmen, always seemed to find the golden key to recovery. Some lost their lives in their monarch's service – another Maurice, for instance, 'a young lusty knight', died from wounds received on the field at Poitiers – but generally they had little ambition for martial glory – nor yet for courtly favours or political power – preferring to be left to enjoy their life as country 'squires', to the care of their lands and buildings, their horses and hounds.

My Day

My most vivid dream is the last of the night's – anarchic, voluptuous and loaded with sensual rewards. Yet this morning, as on many another, I am brutally torn from the midst of its heady swoons by the screaming roar of the first 6 a.m. jet plane nosing lugubriously towards Heathrow. Strange how easily we accept that a couple of dozen Dutch and Belgian businessmen, briefcases snapped on some tiny ambitions, are now given this godlike power to murder a million Londoners' sleep as the machine screams its arrival over the roofs of the city.

The night's end has been decapitated and I am left with a raw, bleeding hour which not even sunrise can honestly cure. Gibbering anxieties press close, looting the ruins. I repel them, given time, and gather strength. But never to return to those grottoes of cosy lusts which the dawn aircraft so blunderingly shattered.

I grope for the bedside transistor. Commercial radio tells me that an articulated lorry has 'jackknifed', blocking both 'carriageways', and that there is a four-mile 'tailback' in both directions. Most mornings in my sheets I hear snippets of some such liturgy – a broken-down van holding up a thousand cars impotently idling on their luxurious Gulf juices. Announced like the weather, or an Act of God. No complaints, unless British Rail is involved.

7 a.m. The light freshens. The plane trees harden in the square. Morning music starts on BBC3 – the tingling antiseptic earwash of Telemann and Scarlatti – and I come awake at last and am healed. Perhaps one of the most civilized ways to be awakened, this. Or by the breathing touch of cat's fur, or a child's fat lips, or the soft, scented fingers of a student nurse from Adelaide.

I make myself some tea and notice again how rankly different it tastes from my weekend Cotswold brew – though the stuff comes from the same branded packet. London tea tastes of metal, the Cotswolds' of beechnuts, the Welsh of a kind of soapy Coke. As I drink my tea I focus wet eyes on my room. Once large, white and clear, I notice how steadily and remorselessly it is becoming walled-in by books, unframed pictures, packets of other people's poems, unarranged antique glasses, oil lamps, chests, broken chairs, crucifixes of straw and wood, magazines, boots, spools of recording tape, bits of sculpture and jars full of swizzle-sticks.

Every morning I notice some new piece of jetsam crowding me in. I remember the days when I could carry all I owned in my two hands. I decide I really must get this stuff sorted out. I know I never will.

As I dress, I hear the BBC concert change to a thick symphonic slab of Schumann. Indigestible as beef at this hour of the day. The orchestra plays it with a kind of cowed exasperation. Every phrase is repeated like hiccoughs.

Almost all my clothes are in this room, scattered around on tables, screens and chairs. Some suits have lain undisturbed for months. I choose from the top of the pile, and switch from Schumann to chatty BBC4. A voice says: 'The time is coming up to 'aff pass tate. The weather in the west will be foggy 'n' hilarious.'

I shave, peering at the pallid face, vulnerable, lopsided, reversed. In it I see the recognizable shade of my father, whose relationship I denied as a boy, and whose mirrored ghost returns each day at this time to haunt me.

Now my daughter, ready for school, thunders in to say goodbye. Clear eyes, tangled hair, cheeks cool as a sliced apple. She bites my lip, punches me hard in the stomach, asks for 10p, then leaves with a lusty shout.

Next a breakfast egg with the post – the latter so different now. No longer the hopes of sudden glories and decorations, gold from unknown admirers, stumbling declarations of love. This morning brings four identical Time/Life circulars, a political pamphlet, a poetry magazine, an invitation to lecture at Huddersfield (sorry, no fee) and a letter from a schoolgirl saying she is doing a project on my autobiography and will I please write and tell her all about my childhood?

It is time now to enter my locked cell, my workroom, the slope-roofed attic looking across to Battersea. The place is small, snug, disorganized and squalid, with a leaking roof, four kinds of peeling wallpaper, a sagging bookcase, cardboard boxes full of wine and papers, first editions signed by friends long dead, or departed to academic stratospheres, continental magazines, pin-ups and worse. This room is encargoed with defeated poems, old manuscripts, beginnings and ends but no middles, but also the rusty medallions of once bright lecheries and loves, photographs, drawings, Krapp's last tapes, cupboard drawers fluttering with letters exhaling the heated breath of girls whom marriage has now chastely cooled or plumped into Titian matrons. Little in this loaded room is ever thrown away. There are no visitors. I am its lone curator.

I cross the littered floor to my desk and sit down. Above my head a green bloom of damp is growing. I blow some Lots Road coal dust off a pile of unanswered letters – which is growing too – and prepare to face the unknown. I hover, unable to say what may emerge this morning from my head's hollow ringing shell. The large desk, of course, is almost invisible under more papers, wine-glasses, boxes of rubber bands, coloured pencils and pens, keys, foreign coins, jugs of scissors, rulers and cigars. This, the freshest point of the hidden day, brings to me a moment of excitement and panic. I find a pencil, and draw some paper towards me. The not quite impossible may be about the happen.

The telephone rings: 'Mr Lee? You won't know me, I'm afraid, but I wonder if I could drop by and have a chat?' Then it's my accountant, expecting some figures. But I've only just sent them. Well, there's a new lot due already. Oh, all right then. I turn back the virgin page and begin to scrabble through my accounts.

Noon: and a luncheon appointment with a young research girl from television. What does she expect of me, I wonder? Will my new safari suit help at all? I put it on. I look like the cad in the old

Tarzan films – the one who always ends up in the crocodile's mouth.

I have a top-floor flat; I run down five flights of stairs and head for King's Road for a taxi; passing Old Church Street (once I had a top flat there, too); also Carlyle Square (and an attic there). I remember yet another attic off the Earl's Court Road, and another, more luxurious, in Tavistock Square. I like the tops of buses, too; and often as a boy I used to climb trees to get away from my family. I wonder why. Pretty obvious really, I suppose.

No taxis in King's Road; it is suffering from a traffic coronary. There is a gentle purring of engines, but nothing moves. I walk towards Sloane Square. The usual exotics crowd the pavements and drift towards me in the stale Kuwait-laden air; fragile, granny-dressed girls, with frail, waxen faces; tough, livid-lipped thirty-year-old teenagers; Shaft-dudes with narrow hips and hats as wide as their shoulders; and chiffon-bloused models showing the last navels of summer. How poised, dotty and jungle-bred they look. They are tall and cool, and walk with a secretive tribal remoteness. I love their style, idiot fineries and confident sexuality. But in private, I wonder, do they weep, stutter, and write pleading little notes to each other?

I walk through them. They see nothing but themselves – not even the stalled traffic – and I remember the King's Road when I first came here. Little greengrocers, shoe-menders, old tobacco-brown pubs, workmen's cafés with kipper-teas for ninepence.

The luncheon is in a Charlotte Street restaurant. It is soft and plush underfoot. The greying Italian waiters have an immaculate air of patronizing politeness mixed with subdued mourning which immediately puts one in one's place. My hostess arrived only two minutes late. She is attractive, charming, with strong eyes and bright, casually ordered hair. The occasion is to be the basis of a literary interview, and the girl flatters me at first as the unknown quantity I still am, takes notes when I speak, asks reverent questions, nods wisely. Gradually, as the meal progresses and she gets to know me better, she develops that faintly distraught and empty look as of one who would rather be anywhere else but here – say with someone much younger or much older, more dashing or more solemn. Finally she puts things right for herself by asking: 'Tell me, do people often say how much you look like Angus Wilson?' Danny Kaye, yes, I think, but never the Old Master. But I say nothing, believing that her asking the question has brought back sense to her meal.

Returning to the flat, I find two telephone messages waiting, both from daily newspapers. What is my favourite recipe? And do I have sexual fantasies? So much easier in the country; they don't ask you, they just do it.

It is teatime. My daughter rushes in from school and slams me again in the stomach. Her face is flushed, hair wilder, eyes excited and absent-looking. She is in love with Christopher Lee, Count Dracula. I say he is a distant cousin of mine. She bites me lightly on the neck.

Sending her off to do her homework, I set about writing some letters, something I am increasingly loath to do. I can never understand such giants as Dickens, D. H. Lawrence, Shaw, who topped off their ten thousand words a day with several dozen sparkling letters. I find it takes me half an hour to compose a message to arrange a gas meter reading. There seem like such an infinite number of ways of saying: 'Tuesday morning; 9.30.'

I must prepare to go out again. I am invited to a small, early party in a publisher's north London back garden. I like to have music while I am changing. There is a Haydn quartet which I find a particularly buoyant sound to go out to. But I put on the wrong tape – spring birdsong recorded from my cottage window over fourteen years ago – blackbirds, cockerels, distant cuckoos, cows, the milkman crunching down the path. All exhalations of that distant life and all of them now dead. No motor cars, buzz saws, juggernauts or planes; just the sound of that quivering, twittering valley, of aimless, unedited time. Hardy could have heard it in all its bountiful boredom. There's nowhere in England you could record it now.

The party is an open-air, walled-in salad of literati and girlfriends; leaves, faces and voices shadowed by an advancing storm.

The dapper publisher wears a bright Malaysian gown, a Midland novelist has a black Russian blouse buttoned up to his white buttoned face. The guest of honour is rouged, excited, charming, red-haired and nearly ninety years old. Blank glasses of Spanish wine dot the garden tables like drying thunder-drops. The flash of cameras alternates with lightning. 'What are you writing now?' 'You can't want for a penny or two.' 'Doing a rewrite, like slicing a stranded whale.' It begins to rain. I share a garden shed with a girl in a light green dress, but it seems that the shed is also the bar. I am asked to leave. I dash for the nearest pub.

Next to the top of a bus there is no creative solitude like that of a pub where one is not known. I approach the bar. The landlord, reading the evening paper, says, 'Well?' and lowers his head again. The starched barmaid, looking over my shoulders, shoves me my drink, takes my pound, and offers my change to a neighbour. Bliss. I sit in a corner and take out my notebook. The limbo of all possible poetry. Crush of strangers, clang of cash registers, mutter of Irish obscenities, all distance and protect me from care or invasion. Phrases and images begin to tick and flicker and run. I fetch another anonymous drink. Then in this supreme privacy of boozy clamour I write effortlessly till closing time.

I walk home and climb the sooty five flights to my flat. It is midnight and I am ready for bed. I have six hours of radiant, supple and nubile dreams before the Dutch businessmen return screaming overhead.

Notes on Marriage

I come from a generation, a class, a habit of behaviours, in which those who married married for life. Like swans and crows and other uncomplicated animals, consorts once chosen reckoned to stay together always. Among the farmers, farm-labourers and mill-workers I grew up with, marriage was not only the inevitable climax to youth, it was also its most solemn occasion, never entered into lightly, often saved up through long years of courtship, because once entered into there was no way out, for divorce in those days was simply unthinkable.

Those lifelong marriages were not without shocks, alarms and desperate entrapments in their early years, but as there was no escape they often improved with age, after the turmoil of raising a family was done. Then would come the quiet running-down into cool retirement, the brief chirruping together like crickets, ending with whist drives, flower shows, mystery coach tours to the sea-side, and in visiting the graves of friends.

Marriages of that kind – and they were in the majority – were not imposed by moral judgments, nor by the Church, but by the lasting realities of survival. Marriage was the only way to safe-guard an uncertain future: it set up a shelter and brought home the food, bred the children and warmed up the mute dark hours. And in a society that suspected anyone who walked alone, marriage was the first claim for protection by the herd.

Such was the pattern of wedlock which surrounded me when I was a boy, but through history and throughout the world, the huge importance of marriage has overshadowed everything else except birth and death. It is probably the most powerful of human instincts, stronger than love or lust, or the desire to make war or money, or even the simple search for security. Because marriage can exist independently of all these passions, yet all are imbedded in it.

Marriage by capture, by dynasty, by family arrangement or broker, or by the casual choice of love – rituals differ but the urge is the same. Marriage by capture must be the oldest and still most popular gambit, which we continue to venerate in old churchyards by the throwing of rice, and by the tying of horseshoes and boots to the back of the getaway car – a symbol of the bride's jealous and pursuing kinsmen.

With the dynastic marriage, so close and sacred were its bonds that only the wedding of brother and sister could hold Ancient Egypt together; while often through the centuries the enlargement of kingdoms and empires was due as much to careful marriage as to outright war.

As for the family-arranged marriage, working either way, by bride-price or by the bride-to-be's dowry, the girl who costs twenty cows is surely that much more cherished, as is she who brings some wealth to her husband, and nothing is thought more likely to keep the marriage bed warm and secure, at least so the theory goes.

Last and most tenuous is marriage for love, which seems strangely to be an invention of the more temperate societies – that reckless taking on of another's life, based on little more than a sudden leap of the heart, a sweep of young limbs, or a glance of the eyes. Here one embarks on a journey with no cargo on board, no maps, and only perishable food.

Throughout the long and complex business of marriage, marrying for love appears to have been a comparatively recent idea. But romantic as we are, or wish to be, it is clear that there are huge dangers in this whimsical habit. From a traditionally arranged marriage love can often grow; marry at love's peak and where do you go but down? Very often it is the last love that lasts the longest, the first that gets early frosted.

Social changes, it is said, don't just happen gradually but in sudden lurches, forward or sideways. The last dozen years, especially in the richer countries of the west, have seen a spontaneous loosening of the marriage ties. The spread of social security, super-gadgetry, processed food and the pill have released a generation from domestic bondage. Sexual relationships now are relaxed and easy and can be slipped in and out of like sleeping-bags. In the past the country peasant required the labour of wife and children to work in his fields and survive. The city peasant of today, nourished on canned food and canned music, needs little else in order to live.

Fidelity, in my youth, was largely a question of bad roads and poor bus services – the crack-up began when we began to move about. Now mobility and overcrowding offer so many alternative choices and proliferation of loves that faithfulness to one person almost suggests dim-wittedness. Societies, classes, races, even religions, have begun to mix, overlap and soak into each other in a way unknown since the days of the Romans.

The birth of modern polygamy had at first a somewhat formal announcement: 'He for the fifth time, she for the third.' A marriage ceremony is no longer necessary when changing one's partner, a line in a gossip column is sacrament enough.

Could one of the reasons that persuades so many to turn away from marriage be that so little remains constant in hope or faith in the future? Is it also an inevitable reaction against legal vows and promises, the wish to share an equality of choice and consent? Certainly there are a multitude of couples living together whose very lack of marriage bonds seems to bind them more strongly.

But brave and easy as these experiments in life-sharing may be, who knows what has been gained or lost? I believe that those who break, even courageously, the ancient laws can still bring down inexplicable disasters upon themselves. The wrath of old gods outraged, with names no longer known or remembered, tears at the fragile happiness of lovers. Most accusing of all are the children, to whom all experiment means disorder, and who are crippled when the family frame is broken. The children, wide-eyed and silent, close to the voice of the gods, they know the laws and they watch and judge. They are also the sacrificial victims of their parents' follies, and every marriage cold-bloodedly, or even light-heartedly, ruined, marks the child with a wound that bleeds for life.

Bernard Shaw once defined marriage as something combining the maximum of temptation with the maximum of opportunity. Although he could have said the same of landlord and pub, marriage of course is more than that. It is the capsule in which one travels some two-thirds of one's life, and which, when stuck to, gives the family a strength and logic no other social arrangement can offer. In spite of our recent juggling with the rules, it is the truth we come back to, the axis on which we balance ourselves, the only cure for that dark curse of sterility and solitude to which man is naturally born.

But to my mind a successful marriage, in spite of its scars and disorders, is an experience timeless as rolling day into night, a state of being where one is free to float among the other's familiar silences, to engage occasionally in the stimulation of combat, but most of all the peace of living with someone who has become one's native country, whose perfect climate is unknown till one leaves it.

End of a Long Summer

In the streets and squares of London now, and in the chill blue misty parks, they are sweeping up the leaves of one of the longest, lushest summers in London's memory. The weather, of course, is one of Britain's oldest tribulations, and one of our oldest jokes. But this year has been no joking matter. Every dream and nostalgia of what the ideal impossible season might be has this time been amply fulfilled, and London has been blessed with a miraculous succession of bright hot days which has set everyone grinning stupidly at each other as though they could just not believe it.

London's usual summer is sweet and piercing short, a thing as temporary as young love. Five days of successive sunshine would call forth front-page headlines in the newspapers, and amazement on all sides. But five or six days were usually the limit. Then the skies would darken and the harsh rains fall, and we would all put on our mackintoshes and feel normal again.

But not so this year. This year has been unbelievable, historic, something to write poems about. Not just five days of it, this time, but five times five and double that again. Morning after morning we have woken up to see a bright and steady sunshine gilding the streets of this ordinarily grey city. Day after day we have watched a tropical sun climb from the smoky horizons of unclouded blue. Evening after evening we have been able to walk in the warm amber light of perfect summer sunsets and to feel a mysterious assurance that the next day would be as good.

It has all meant a great difference to us in this city. For one thing, life has been able to come out much more into the open. Schoolchildren have been able to run half-naked in the parks, their chubby bodies turning brown as country apples. After work, during the long soft evenings, we were able to lean from wide-open windows and to get to know our neighbours – often for the first time in our lives. Café tables with brightly chequered cloths – a most un-English sight – began to appear on the broader pavements of Chelsea, Kensington and the Edgware Road, where lovers could sit in the golden air, drinking sweet coffee and gazing at the unfamiliar sky. Even that most conservative of characters, the British workman, often forsook the shadowy interior of his pub to drink his black beer in the open street.

Yes, it has been a poem of a summer: ice cream was never creamier nor more desirable, the pigeons never fatter nor drowsier, the policemen in their tight blue suits never more breathless. A voluptuous enchantment seemed suddenly to encompass puritan London and it opened like a rose. Suddenly everyone began painting their houses. Rooftops and window-ledges dripped with flowers. Gorgeously designed coffee houses, full of parrots, monkeys and exotic plants, began to spring up in every street. And shopgirls in vivid cotton dresses seemed to spawn like butterflies on the pavements, each one more beautiful than the last. Indeed, this summer has brought something like a visual revolution to London life, and London, during the past three months, has seemed at times almost like a Mediterranean city.

But London cannot be, nor would ever wish to be, anything but itself. It has taken this happy weather to its heart, felt the better for it, and translated it into a fresher pattern of its own enjoyment. A mixture of old and new is what is most typical of modern London, and one of the symbols or focal points of this contemporary spirit can be found on the south bank of its busy river, in the new Pleasure Gardens at Battersea Park. I want to tell you about this place, because it seems to me to embody something that is significant to the light side of London life.

Battersea Park Gardens were born some four years ago as part of the great 1951 Exhibition, and nothing quite like it has ever happened in London before. In conception this pleasure ground is revolutionary, a thing of delicate and exotic fancy, with echoes of

Kubla Khan and Shakespeare's *A Midsummer Night's Dream*. Though planned as a temporary residence, it has already become one of London's summer institutions, and this year it has come especially into its own.

Sensual, lyrical and quite unashamedly devoted to pleasure, each year, now, it re-opens with the spring, lies free for us all throughout the summer, and, with the falling of leaves, is locked away until the following spring. And so, because I wished to say goodbye to the summer we have had, in a place which I identify with London's summer, I went to the Garden the other night, on the night of its annual closing. And a bright scene met my eyes.

The Garden with its flowers, fountains, pavilions and golden spires was enclosed in the ripe warm light of an autumn evening. The bridges leading across the river, and the river bank itself, were strung with lights like coloured fruit. Music whispered from the tops of painted turrets, and floodlit fountains turned languid jets of water against the sky. Here and there, on the tops of fretted columns, sculptured bamboo figures stood on tiptoe like dancers engraved in light. Mobile waxworks laughed shakily from among the trees. An avenue of small shops, gaily striped like the tents of Arabs, offered for sale all kinds of pretty merchandise. Nearby, in a red-bricked open-air theatre, a circus with ponies and painted clowns played to a gathering of enchanted children. In cages among the flowers were screaming parrots, peacocks, pheasants and birds of paradise. And at the far end of the Garden, bright and brassy beneath the smoking chimneys of Battersea Power Station, the Funfair awaited our pleasure with roundabouts, rifle ranges, coconut shies, sausage stalls, switchback railways and lighted wheels revolving in the sky.

It was the last night of summer, and the Funfair was a snare of light and excited voices. A bright-eyed crowd, light-footed with pleasure, was there in festive force. There were mothers with leaping children, proud fathers laden with prizes, sweet-faced shopgirls nibbling doughnuts, Indian students in vivid sarees, laughing Negroes, grave Chinese – all the multitudinous and varied elements of a typical London crowd, and all out to have a good time.

Some were shooting bottles, throwing darts, playing skittles, firing arrows; others were screaming on swings and roundabouts or sedately eating plates of vinegary seafood.

So the gay night passed. Under a rusty moon on the banks of the liquid Thames, it was a fine end to our long summer. The children trundled homewards at last, dragging their footsteps, exhausted with pleasure. People drove singing away on buses. The lovers lingered awhile under the dying lights. Then the gates were finally closed, and winter officially began.

That winter must come, of course we know. But fortified by this splendid summer London, this year, is ready for it.

Autumn

Harvest Festival

Last weekend, while on a visit from London, I struck gold in the Stroud valley. For chance, and the coincidence of time and weather, conspired together to show me the district at its autumn best. The sloping fields and crested beechwoods were bathed in a rich sunlight more radiant than the airs of Greece: apples and pears dropped like gifts into my hands, and the clear stone cottages shone like temples upon their hills and hollows.

Never had I seen a landscape more tender, more inexhaustible in its variety, more jewel-like in its reflections of sky, leaf, stone and water. Since leaving the district, more than twenty years ago, I have travelled through some forty countries, but I know now that the green crumpled valleys around Stroud are unique in their beauty of contour, intimacy, pastoral charm, and in the shining light that fills them.

My visit fell at a perfect time, and for two days I walked through the honey-coloured valleys, contrasting their September glories with my earlier recollections of them. And in spite of my incurable leaning towards nostalgic excess, the district had never seemed more beautiful than it did now, glowing with the ripeness of yet another harvest.

Then on the third day, which was Sunday morning, I suddenly heard hymn-singing from a church. As a boy, living in Slad village, harvest festival had always seemed to me to be the crown of the year, an occasion of richness and thanksgiving, when one felt closer to the mystery and benevolence of the earth than at any other time. So on this glittering, chrysanthemum-scented morning, I went eagerly into the church, seeking the ancient magic I remembered.

It was a good service, and had obviously been planned with devotion. But it differed somewhat from the harvest festivals I had attended in my village days. Some of the changes were even for the better. For instance, the choir was big, well rehearsed and sang excellently. And to the traditional benches of men and boys were now added rows of cap-and-gowned young girls joining their sweet but different presences to the once inviolate harmony of males. This, I felt, was an improvement: but they also sang hymns I'd never heard of, taken from the hymn-books of an edition much later than mine, and this left me in the cold. More significant still, the choir far outnumbered the congregation, which was composed of one old verger, a spruce young sidesman, a few mothers and children, but no obvious harvesters anywhere. But by modern standards this was not too serious, for I know many churches where the parson alone outnumbers both choir and congregation.

As for the decorations, they had been made with care and taste, but were somewhat restrained in quantity. A dozen tomatoes were arranged across the altar, and in front of it stood a loaf of bread and two handfuls of short-strawed wheat. In a corner lay a bunch of carrots, three onions and a pot of homemade jam. Elsewhere were jars of Michaelmas daisies, strings of red creepers, and a marrow.

'The valleys stand so thick with corn that they do laugh and sing!' sang the choir. Listening to these happy words, I thought this is true, so they do, and these gifts are their proper symbols. But looking around these handsome urban walls I could not help recalling, inevitably, Slad Church and the harvest festivals of my youth.

History and progress has changed the emphasis of our lives, and it is too late to complain. But how heavily and abundantly was our small church loaded then. The cream of the valley was used to decorate it. To pass through its door, those festivals ago, was like crawling into a cornucopia, a laden granary, a grotto of bright flowers. Its familiar walls seemed totally obscured by the gifts we had culled from our brimming fields and gardens. Four great stocks of wheat stood up before the altar, together with round ornamental loaves as big as cartwheels. The altar itself was piled with golden apples. Bunches of grapes, from the squire's own vines, hung blue from the lips of the pulpit. The fat round pillars which divided the church wore skirts of barley and cowls of yellow flowers. In the deep window-ledges, matted with leaves and moss, sat mountains of pears and plums and gigantic marrows. And thick on the floor, wherever there was space, lay scrubbed and shining vegetables.

But perhaps the richest harvest of all was the congregation. Everybody from the valley was there, from shuffling greybeards to tottering babes. Farmers sat square in their hairy tweeds. Young cowmen choked in their tight cravats. There were mothers and maidens, dads and boys, spinsters, bachelors and cranky hermits – but all had come to give thanks for harvest, and almost all had some claim on the land. And as we sat in our pews, waiting for the service to begin, our eyes sought proudly the gifts we had brought, the pick of our year's husbandry: and a mysterious excitement, as old as man's sojourn on the earth, began to well up within us.

I remember one particular occasion which perfectly sums up this almost pagan feeling. I was sitting beside my brother Tony, who was then about three years old. It was the first harvest festival he had ever attended, but he'd heard much about it and his expectation was huge. The air was thick with the odours of fruit and flowers. The choir was fidgeting in the doorway, ready to start its procession. Tony gazed round the church with rapt and glistening eyes. Then, in a moment of utter silence, just before the organ cracked into its first hymn, he asked in a loud ecstatic voice: 'Is there going to be drums, eh? Is there going to be drums?' . . .

It was a natural question, innocent and true. For neither drums, nor cymbals, nor trumpets of brass would have seemed out of place in those days. As it was, we bawled out thanksgivings at the tops of our voices; and even when we had to sing, 'all is safely gathered in', knowing full well that one of Farmer Lusty's fields was still rotting in the rain, this minor discrepancy didn't seem important. What was important was the feeling of magic that we, living intimately with the earth, always experience when we joined to praise, once again, its everlasting bounty.

That was how it was. It is not so any more. But the ghosts of those old hymns sing through us still, though the bill of our gratitude must now be expressed in things other than wheaten sheaves. Meanwhile, the grassy combes and wooded crests of the Stroud valleys do not change, nor their rioting flowers, placid silences, nor the purple distances seen from their hills. And in spite of all the power and richness of modern life, it is here I most wish to be, where the landscape offers its endless festivals to the eye and to the spirit, perpetual harvests.

On Craftsmen

We are a starved society living in the midst of plenty. Our possessions are many, our serenities few.

If we look at objects fashioned by the hands of craftsmen, we instinctively recognize something we need, something we may almost have forgotten existed any more – something designed to keep us human. For the handmade object is one of the last visible defences of humanism left to us, and the craftsman ministers to our most basic spiritual needs.

The materials he works in – wood, stone, clay, iron, living wools and natural hides – are still those divine materials of the earth for which there are many substitutes today, but no replacements. His products are the result not of the juddering steel press, die-stamp and reeking chemical synthesis of mass production, but of human skills and judgments which have filtered down into these pages, into this moment, through unbroken generations of eyes and hands.

It is this we are in danger of losing forever – the virtue of the handmade object, whose making yields to no factory speed-up, but is the loving product of the master craftsman, of silence and slow time. In robbing man of the use of his hands, mechanization mutilates his spirit also.

One of the most monstrous heresies of our time is that vandalism is permissible in advances in the name of that hideous and unholy trinity; speed, efficiency, economy! So the naked pylons straddle our beech woods, the crude entrails of the powerhouse erupt by the village church, and those ghastly palings of wire and concrete strangle ten thousand miles of our roads and fields. The use of such shabby materials may save shillings in upkeep, while meanwhile whole landscapes are permanently corrupted.

It is in the face of such influence that these craft goods are so important. They are no cosy reminders of the past, but issue a revolutionary challenge to the mechanistic squalor in which we live.

'Look at us,' they say. 'We are expensive; we took a long time to make. But we are beautiful, and will last for years. And there is not another one quite like us in the world, for we are made by hand.'

Letter from Britain

The evenings in London now are chill and mysterious. In the sky and streets there is a blue autumnal haze. The last flowers of summer have been cleared from the parks, and the Government window boxes in Whitehall smoulder with gold chrysanthemums. It is October; and as the first breath of winter begins to kindle the fires and boilers in a thousand shops, offices and public buildings, London settles down under its smoke to prepare for the coming cold.

And London, with its lights, fires, smoke and multitudes, can be a cosy place in winter – much cosier than rainswept fields and dripping woods. And it's not only man that finds it so. For this is the time of year when a strange visitation begins to occupy the heart of this great city – a comparatively recent visitation, but mysterious, wild and un-citylike.

Any evening now, if you walk up from the Thames Bank into Trafalgar Square – that broad space of fountains where Nelson's Column stands – you'll hear, above the roar of the traffic, a rushing of wings and a bright high squealing of countless chattering tongues. They are sounds that will stop you in your tracks, and as you stare, amazed, at the buildings and the sky around you, you will see, not one, but tens of thousands of birds. For Trafalgar Square has become a gigantic roost of starlings – in fact, during the last few years it has become one of the biggest roosts in the country.

Together with a million other city workers, I find strange food for thought in this nightly apparition. For though this district teems with human workers in the daytime, very few people sleep here at night. Night is the signal for a great migration; in a couple of hours buses and trains carry the whole million of us away to the suburbs, where our homes are; the shops and offices are locked, and the streets become empty. It is then that the practical starling takes over, coming in from the country, where he feeds, to occupy, each night, the roofs and walls and window-ledges of the buildings we have deserted.

It might almost seem to be an ideal arrangement, designed to make the most of this small and crowded island. Except that the starlings consulted no one about it, and carry no baggage, pay no room-rent, and display, in fact, an easy-going anarchy that is the envy of all and the despair of the city cleaners.

Starlings are a bright and cocky breed of bird, and their international relations are in very good order. Every year, great flocks from Norway, Sweden, Denmark, Germany, even the icy plains of Russia, slip smoothly across the frontiers and come to winter in Britain. They set up great roosting grounds in the countryside, but seldom visit the towns. It is the British breed, accustomed to the cosier sanctuaries of the place, who have taken to roosting here in London. And because they have so increased in numbers during the past few years, it's not just the occasional treeful in the park that we see now, but buildings blackened with twittering throngs that even the most down-to-earth of city-dwellers must close his umbrella now and stare up at them and wonder.

And it is with a peculiar mixture of wonderment, half-pleased, half-worried, that he views this gigantic occupation of his man-made buildings. It is as though the world of birds had suddenly broken loose from its remote and traditional settlements and decided to muscle in on man's own territory. It brings to the Londoner the same feeling of uneasy excitement that he might get if a herd of Dartmoor ponies were to take over a block of flats, or if swarms of wasps suddenly began to leave their nests and settle in all the letter boxes in the town.

In my case, so far as the starlings are concerned, something very like this seems to be happening here. The other night, instead of hurrying home as usual, I stayed for an hour to watch. Let me try to give you a picture of what I saw. As the sun went down from a pale-blue autumn sky, swift scurrying little flocks of birds began to come in from every point of the compass. I stood below Nelson's Column, and they came in low over the roofs in tens, twenties and thirties, like handfuls of black pennies, like spots before the eyes. Then, because the evening was fine, or just for the fun of it, they began to join forces and circle above the Square; massing, dividing, merging again; climbing and swooping, but in such miraculous order, and in such numbers, that the eye was made dizzy with their rhythmic complications. They swept the sky like bursts of grape-shot, they bombarded Nelson's statue with black confetti, they settled thick on rooftops, then blew away like dust. Londoners, homeward bound from work, missed their buses and almost got run over, standing to see the sky above them all veiled with birds like a storm that never broke. And still the birds massed and multiplied in the air; condensing, one moment, into a small black cloud, then spreading out into a vast floating web so tenuous at times it seemed to cover the whole sky.

What I saw then, you can see every night. It is always the same. As darkness gathers, the flocks break up and drop down to their roosts. Then the face of the National Gallery, St Martin's Church, Admiralty Arch, and all the shipping offices down Cockspur Street are suddenly veiled as though with antic Spanish lace. The slender scaffolding above Charing Cross Station is threaded as though with beads, and the trees in the Embankment Gardens sag with dark loads like fruit.

It is then that their chatter starts, and the noise is terrific. The buildings squeal and twitter with it, and it rises steadily in excitement till the sound of the traffic is swamped. And, it has to be admitted, it is a happy noise; while the birds sit in their tight rows along the eaves and window-ledges, feathers sparkling, heads turning, wings folding and bodies settling for the night.

With the coming of darkness, the electric advertisements glow and flicker, and the lovely fountains by Nelson's lions rise and fall in showers of floodlit silver. And still the starlings sit and chatter, loving the lights, as excited as children. I can't think when they get any rest at all. I was coming home quite late from the theatre the other night, and they were still at it. I stood and listened, and a stout motherly old lady in a bus queue nearby cocked up her head and gave them a stern but affectionate glance. 'Them birds,' she said. 'They ought to be asleep.'

And that, I suppose, is the attitude of most of us towards them – affection, mixed with concern and wonder. The sanitary authorities, of course, feel less indulgent, and wish they'd never come. In fact they have thought up all sorts of devices to discourage the birds, from nets and supersonic rays to nightly alarms of flares and banging rockets.

But here they still are. Every night, as we go home, they take over. And as they shower down out of the evening sky we are stirred by strange far-off instincts at the sight of them, reminding us of other worlds and other ways. They suggest, among other things, how slight are the frontiers still between modern man and nature. For if starlings can occupy so spontaneously the heart of a city, might not man just as easily go back to roost in trees? 'Just think of that,' says the clerk to himself as he climbs to the top of his bus. And for a moment there is an old primeval glitter in his eye.

Return to Stroud Secondary
Modern School

I woke in the cold dark of the November morning and began fumbling miserably for my clothes. A point of pain in my groin, which I'd not felt since boyhood, started replaying the old excuses for not going at all.

I'd have preferred to revisit my village school, but that had been scrapped several years ago. So I borrowed my daughter's satchel and set off for the old secondary modern – not the usual three-mile run through the rain in dripping shorts and split boots, nor the occasional rusty grind on the family bicycle, nor yet the hot flesh-and-rubber creak of the bus more recently laid on by the council, but, for the first and last time, by car.

The handsome redbrick complex of education islands still lies athwart Stroud's western meadows. Architecturally and by sexes they remain an archipelago, and are now academically joined.

Wishing, like Odysseus, to retrace the final stage on foot, I asked to be set down at the end of the lane. The tuckshop on the corner, once a casket of jewelled sugars, was now a bulldozed and rubbled space. I slouched up the lane. It was 8.45 a.m. Morosely I stared at the backs of the schoolgirls' legs. What I remembered to have been encased in thick black lisle was now dipped in the sheerest nylon.

I approached my school's iron-toothed and engulfing gate. How often, unprepared and unannealed, had I been sucked in and chewed up here? Half a lifetime later, how would I be received? As a middle-aged freak or total stranger? A small boy approached me with an armful of books. ''Allo, Laurie,' he nodded, and passed on.

The assembly bell rang and my scalp immediately prickled with old anxieties and compulsions to obey. I hurried with the other boys to the Assembly Hall where we paraded in unnatural silence. A murmur arose from somewhere. 'You'll not be told again!' thundered the chaplain. It seemed that it was me who was doing the talking.

The Headmaster arrived; the masters lined up by the wall; somebody hit the piano hard. The Head prayed for the unsuccessful; then we sang 'To Be a Pilgrim', during which a polite boy lent me an upside-down hymn-book.

Since my time, the main school had grown by a kind of cellular action, adding mini-expanding huts and Terrapins. Which class would I like to sit in on, they asked – French? German? Physics? All of them unheard of in my day; I chose English.

I would have preferred to slip in unnoticed and to follow my usual grubby evasions – drawing nudes, scribbling verse or just dozing. But as I entered, the whole class rose to its feet like guardsmen and the master shoved me up front where he could keep an eye on me.

He was a gifted man, with a prowling, challenging style, snapping out questions like a prosecuting counsel, but he managed to keep the class in a state of unrepressed eagerness, all crackling with impatient answers.

It was at this school, in this lesson, at the age of these boys, that my formal introduction to English ended. This morning we did some spelling, and I still got 'achievement' and 'protein' wrong: then, after tackling a verse of Tennyson, I asked to be excused.

I headed straight for the locker room – that boot-smelling, crushed-grass refuge with its original wooden lockers still gaping like raided tombs. The whole school, battened down to its morning tasks, was humming drowsily like a coastal oil tanker. With ears cocked for that always possible and fatal footfall of exposure, I crouched in my old corner and knocked off a couple of beers.

Reckless now, with the empties rattling about in my satchel, I went brazenly into the Headmaster's study. In no way impressed by the empty gesture of bravado, he asked the chaplain to pour me a cup of coffee.

Together they had dug out for my inspection the old school

logbook, opened at the appropriate page. In the faded handwriting of earlier, less amiable headmasters, it recorded the dates of my arrival and departure from the school. 'Term completed', it added lamely, but between the dates nothing, no honours or failures, nor even a ripple of scandal. Indeed, I had left no mark on that school, not even my initials scratched on a wall. I had been a hider, a watcher, a fence-sitter, a no-risk-taker, committing myself to life's embrace only during after-school hours. So this morning, to make up for it, not only had I gone swigging liquor in the locker room, I also went, uninvited, and rang the handbell for break . . .

Sacred moment of power, reserved only for prefects, a dizzy status I never achieved. Now, at my signal, lessons stopped, doors flew open, masters sped to their hideouts, boys streamed out on the tarmac. I joined the boys for football but we fell about too much, so they pinned me against the wall. 'Give us your autograph, then.' Well-chewed biros were offered, but they seemed to have nothing to write on except the flyleaves of hymn-books. I found myself scribbling: 'Bless Kevin', 'Praise Keith', 'May Grace Fall on Garry', or 'Pray for Laurie Lee, a Sinner'.

'You ought to be writing gags for Morecambe and Wise,' sniffed Garry, snatching back his battered ballpoint.

After break I slipped into one of those supreme temples of our maleness, the stand-up WCs pitched against the High School wall – magical and inexplicable siting, from which one could hear the throb of the girls at their games, or watch the sweet curve of their netballs rise above the sheet-iron fence.

I went next to the History lesson. My original desk was still there, and I was allowed to cram myself into it. I recognized the ribbed grains of the wood, like old dried kippers, the blots and knife-whittlings, and the claw-marks of boredom. The last time I'd been here we were doing Assurbanipal of Nineveh, this morning it was Hammurabi of Babylon; the boys were at least a dynasty ahead of me and were manifestly enjoying Hammurabi's codes of law – all about knocking people's eyes out and keeping women in their place.

I shared the first sitting at lunch with the Headmaster and his lady, and were served by a bright extrovert who claimed I'd been to school with his great-uncle. He had a plaster cast on his left hand inscribed 'I Love Julie', with other mottoes. Alas, we had nothing like such style in our day.

We didn't have such excellent food, either; we brought our own, wrapped in brown paper – sugared margarine sandwiches or perhaps a crinkled apple. Some of the better-off farmers' sons might bring chicken bones or cake, and what they threw away we fought for.

As the schoolday gradually closed for me I began to count how much and how little had changed. Rooms and corridors, pictures on the walls, even the masters were the same (with their jackets and flannels and enthusiastic, half-despairing energies). But the boys were a new breed altogether. My mates had been a lumpy, rough, rather grimy lot, all shapes and sizes, like potatoes grown among stones. Today's pupils were polite, witty, noisy, well dressed and many with an extraordinary smooth beauty which we did not have. They had a dash and a confidence too, being now part of the grammar school next door and having access to a sacred turf we were never allowed to tread.

But they'd been robbed of one thing, I thought. When the day's lessons were over, buses would sweep them instantly back to their tea and television. They would not know, as we had, the languors of the slow walk home, with a couple of girls at last freed to join us and the pleasures of climbing the valley together, on foot, throughout the seasons, while pursuing the endless after-school investigation of each others' minds and bodies.

The Recurring Image

Of all the aberrations that propel the driving force of love, one of the most mysterious is that of the recurring image. Who could it be, this chosen one who constantly haunts you, who you follow in a lifelong pursuit, this face and figure that obliterates all others and whose magic works only for you?

A friend of mine, comfortably married for years, suddenly left his wife and went halfway round the world to marry another who could have been her twin.

Miss Elizabeth Taylor seems always to wed the same dynamic gold-digger, Miss Brigitte Bardot to dote on the same languid youth, while Tommy Manville's thirteen brides, when you study their photographs, are as identical as a row of knickerbocker glories.

What can be the source of this image which enters one's heart and imagination with all the regularity of the visiting moon? We seek it and hold it, marry and remarry it, or just love and leave it to search for it again. But where, in the beginning, did this phantom spring from? Obviously the ideal can approach one from many separate paths, uninvited, unsuspecting, unknowing.

It could be the quite ordinary figure whose chance appearance coincided with a moment of first sexual arousal. Or the never-to-be-forgotten ghost that sleep chose as a companion to share one's first erotic dream. Or the search could be for a girl whose face most closely resembled that rosecheeked schoolboy whose sweeping eyelashes and fresh-scrubbed innocence first stopped the heart and taught one what beauty was.

Although many of us have been spared this particular fixation, most have witnessed its effect on others. Often with some surprise or even cynical resignation: 'Can't think what he sees in her, myself'; 'Surely not another gamekeeper? – or ski instructor or Swedish starlet or priest?' 'What a very odd couple, my goodness.'

We may not understand it, but it would be wrong to discount it, for the recurring image is one of love's most permanent guardians. On whoever's head the flickering flame may fall, and no matter how often it may dance from one to another, the lover will recognize it and follow it steadfastly in a paradoxical act of lifelong fidelity.

It can begin with that special look, line of cheek and shoulder, the silhouette that stops one dead in the street.

It can drag you out of a train and force you to take the one going in the opposite direction because of a face seen in the carriage window.

At its most extreme, it can make one leave home, change jobs, even change one's country. Its force can be so personal no one else will be aware of it, yet it can entirely direct and rule one's life.

In my case I have been split by two opposing obsessions, occupying two sides of my nature and reverse sides of my fate. They may have sprung from dreams, from inheritance, or something going back to the doorways of childhood, but I recognized them first at my village school. They were as different from each other as noon from midnight, but they have kept me perilously balanced between them.

One was pretty gold-haired Rosie with her tight-petalled curls, sticky mouth and air of portable sweetshops. The recurrence of this healthy, romping, innocently carnal little blonde has been with me like perpetual summer.

The other I first saw in the pub-keeper's daughter – something sinuous, slant-eyed, oriental or Celtic, with hair as black as slate or the oils of Oman. The Rosie image has always been one of scampering pleasure, of a kind of creamy pastoral wantonness. But from what deep crevice of the mind did the dark one rise, that she should so incessantly command my senses?

I remember the pub-keeper's daughter and the first sign she gave me, that blank almost basilisk stare, and the brooding hold of her body, with me on the school wall, watching, struck dumb to the marrow, knowing that something terrible and everlasting had started. She was the first imprinting of that symbol which I have constantly met since, in flashing glimpses or in longer possessions under different names and in different places, in India, Spain, Cornwall, London.

Looking back, I see this recurring image as one of the preservatives of love, a succession of occupations by a spirit unique to herself and to which all one's passions belong. I don't say that this way happiness lies (believing mere happiness to be one of life's shallower experiences).

This hovering visitation need not always be a physical presence. It can be a quality of mind, a way of regarding the world. But for me, trapped all my days in my double helix, slowly spiralling between sunlight and shades, the stronger and most compelling has always been the dark one, her panther tread, voice full of musky secrets, her limbs uncoiling on beds of moonlight.

Why this should have been my allotment I shall never discover now, but whoever she is, wherever she came from, in spite of her treacheries and long dismembering knives, she has kept me alive beyond the dreams of apathy, and honoured me with a love more than normal love.

Not everyone requires, nor seeks, the stimulus of the recurring image. They are content to be without directions. But for those of us who are branded by this particular mark, at least we know where we're going.

We are going, as it were, on a series of seasonal journeys, the climax of which is simply returning home.

The Street Where I Grew Up

Home for most of my youth was a thick-walled Cotswold cottage in the village of Slad, near Painswick. There were seven children, three inherited from Father's first wife who died young. In those days, cottages were called by the family name, so ours was Lee's Cottage.

I was dumped into the long grass, aged three, and left grizzling among the beetles and grasshoppers. I lived there until I was nineteen and left home to see the world and make my fortune. I knew every flower, weed, stoat, badger and bird. Not many people know that in Slad the blackbirds sing with a Gloucestershire accent. When I returned after twenty years' exile I heard the blackbirds' accent and knew I was home.

Our cottage looked up a steep bank to a road that was built in the eighteenth century. This road was our social centre and playground, where we'd spin tops, roll marbles, play five-stones and chase the girls. There was no danger from traffic because there wasn't any. If a cart came, we'd see it half a mile away advancing in clouds of white dust. It was a great event when the wagoners drove by, bringing timber from the woods and pulled by as many as six horses.

My billowing sisters used to run up and down like butterflies, and the village women climbed up their steps and gathered in inscrutable, garrulous bunches to gossip about scandals, disasters and love affairs, clicking their tongues and rehearsing the age-old histories of village life. I only have to list the names – Brown, Green, Webb, White – monosyllabic names which were derived from wool-weavers, for me to be transported back to that intense intimacy which I shared with that community.

Lee's Cottage was, and still is, shaped like a T. Part of it was inhabited by two old ladies who we called ''er up top' and ''er down under'. They were very cantankerous towards each other. One would hop up and down on her floor to create a disturbance and the other would bang on the ceiling with a broom.

I remember watching one as she combed her hair and saying – you know what kids are like – 'You're going bald, gran.' Cackling, she replied: 'I got more than 'er down under, the old faggot, she's as bald as a potato root.'

My mother wasn't very good at cooking. We all crammed into the kitchen for porridge, lumpy baked cabbage, bread and marge with sugar on it and lentil soup which was like eating hot, rusty buttons. On Sundays we sometimes had a rabbit which a neighbour gave us.

At the village school I learned poetry that I've never forgotten. Neither have I forgotten the girl whose hand I held as we sat at our desks, and who was the gateway into the extended world of sexual awareness.

But I have something rather shameful to confess which I've never admitted before. When I was eleven, the Royal Society for the Protection of Birds and Trees organized an essay competition, and our teacher told us to choose a bird or tree, study it and write an essay. I found my prize-winning effort, called 'The Dabchick', among some old papers the other day. Written in copperplate hand-writing it starts: 'The Dabchick or Dipper haunts streams and ponds and is called Dab or Dipper because it dabs or dips its bill in the water . . .' And from this point onwards I am cheating, making it up, as I describe the nest-building habits and the way it feeds its young etc. I certainly never consulted any books; not a word is accurate, yet I got a medal for it, presented by a teacher with moist eyes.

My father left us when I was tiny and I always hoped that he would come back. I still have all the love letters he wrote to his first wife, which my mother kept. She treated her predecessor with a certain amount of reverence – obviously you can forgive someone who dies young. But I don't forgive my father. I remember him coming home when I was about eight and Mother saying, 'Oh Reg, can't we make it up?' and I knew with icy certainty that this would never happen. Mother used to dress in her best silks and play the piano on summer evenings, and I thought that this was the time he should have come down the path and back to her. I knew I ought to embrace her as she played, but I never did.

When war came, Father bought himself a bulletproof vest, but never saw active service, and after the war he claimed pension money. He'd send a form which my headmaster would sign. One day I was asked what my father's wounds or disabilities were, and, as I didn't know, I asked Mother who said that he was 'partially incapacitated' which, I now suppose, meant 'nerves'. So the next time I took the form, I said to my headmaster: 'I understand that my father is partially *decapitated*.'

When I was eleven, I wanted to learn the violin. There was a violin hanging on the kitchen wall but no bow. Mother wrote to Father asking if he could buy me a bow, but there was a very slow response. Meanwhile, I attended lessons, learning the fingering but without a bow. I still have my music teacher's report which says: 'Lack of a bow has spoilt Laurie's chances at playing the violin', which is rather like Nureyev's teacher writing on his report: 'Lack of feet has spoilt his chances of becoming a dancer.'

In those days, the seasons affected us. Winter and summer were different countries. During the long languorous twilights of summer, we kids were outside playing chase and hide-and-seek throughout the length of the valley until – and I know I'm sounding a bit idyllic – the final setting of the sun.

In winter, we took refuge from the elements by gathering together in our kitchens, heated by brushwood fires, lighting candles and oil lamps and sitting round sketching, singing, chatting, my sisters sewing; no wireless or TV to distract us. We led marooned lives, marooned by nature and by lack of transport. What it all boils down to is the growth of my consciousness, of being the height of grass, dominated by beetles and birds; and later, people, seasons and emotions. Slad village was the centre of my universe.

These days, I sometimes walk past Lee's Cottage, now called Rose Bank. It looks much the same and is known locally as Laurie Lee's Cottage, though I haven't been inside for sixty-one years and though my present cottage is further along the village. Some Londoners moved in twenty years ago and no doubt found the garden a tangle of redcurrants and syringa. They have been greatly pestered by pilgrims who have read *Cider with Rosie*, who stare in the windows and take snaps. I know that they have found living there a bit of an imposition. When my book began to sell, a chap up the road, a bit of a rascal, said: 'If I'd known then what I know now I'd have bought that cottage and opened it up for cream teas', and I thought to myself: 'I've made it, at last.'

The road is now a racetrack for the local Ford Sierras and children can't cross it. Every cottage has one or two bloated blowfly motor cars encroaching in their gardens, and at the time of day when women once congregated to natter about the joys and griefs that reflected the history of that small community, people now stay indoors to enjoy a second-hand history: *The Archers*, *Emmerdale*, *Neighbours*, written by manipulative scriptwriters in their city offices. I don't want to sound an old curmudgeon, but soap operas are no substitute for real community life.

King Charles Lane is still there, where King Charles came through on his way to relieve the Siege of Gloucester, and so is the oak tree, called the King's Oak, which I used to climb as a boy. The sun and the moon still rise behind a certain clump of trees. You can look across the valley and see fields and hedges which have been undisturbed since Elizabethan days. There's still the hill with two great quarries from which came the stones that have built most of the walls and cottages in this valley.

The three-centuries-old Woolpack Inn is still the village focal point, though these days it has a 'Cider with Rosie' bar. I was an imaginative lad, but I could never have foreseen such a turn-up for the books – in fact, my books are sold in the pub.

Pupils who are studying *Cider with Rosie* often arrive with their teachers to be driven round the village in minibuses for a *Cider with Rosie* tour. I was sitting outside The Woolpack and two young schoolgirls said: 'Excuse me, sir, can you tell us where Laurie Lee is buried?'

To which I replied, 'You'll find him buried in the public bar most days.'

But it gave me a great shiver of mortality because the church-yard is just across the road from the pub. My mother is buried there and a sister who died at four, and I expect to be buried there myself.

I want to go back. It's my valley and I want to be returned to the soil and the roots from which I was born.